D1564427

CHANGE OF
Fortune

VINCENT HOSANG *with* ALEX LEE

To: Hana Namkung

Best Regards
Vincent Hosang
Nov 3. 2018

CHANGE OF
Fortune

How One Determined Immigrant
Built His American Dream

VINCENT HOSANG *with* ALEX LEE

© 2016 Vincent HoSang

All rights reserved. This book or any portion thereof may not be reproduced or used in any manner whatsoever without the express written permission of the author or publisher, except for the use of brief quotations in a book review.

Printed in the United States of America

First Printing, 2016

ISBN: 978-0-99749-610-9

Library of Congress Control Number: 2016912700

Edited by: Kirkus Reviews (Kirkus' Book Editing Services)

Published by: BookBaby Book Publishing

To my parents, Henry and Nukelyn HoSang, who instilled in me the value of hard work.

To my wife, Jeanette, who took care of our family, too often on her own, while I took care of business; and to our four beautiful children, who never complained.

To my brother, and friend, King for his vision, and to all my siblings for their incredible tenacity.

To the Caribbean Food Delights and Royal Caribbean Bakery families, for showing me that "no man is an island."

Finally, to my son Brian, in whose loving memory I dedicate the story of my journey.

A C K N O W L E D G M E N T S

My deepest appreciation goes to those who carved out time from their busy lives to help me with this book. First on the list, family—my wonderful wife, Jeanie, son, Damian, daughters, Sabrina, and Simone. Next, dearest friends and associates—Hollis "Barry" Levy; the Most Hon. P. J. Patterson, O.N., O.C.C., P.C., Q.C.; Dr. Basil Bryan, O.D.; Aston Lue; Martin Cybul, R.A., A.I.; Brad Kreinces, C.P.A., C.G.M.A.; Irwine Clare, Sr., O.D.; Conroy Allison; Jeff Barnes, Esq.; Raquel Pascual; Charles Chung; Rev. Calvin McIntyre; and the Very Rev. Fr. Richard Ho Lung. Thank you, everyone, for walking down memory lane with me, and helping to breathe life into this personal project.

To Janice Julian, Kathleen Barker, and Sabrina HoSang Jordan, thank you, team, for taking on the laborious task of going through the drafts with me several times over. To Simone HoSang, thank you for your spot-on critique of the book's cover design. A second round of thanks and appreciation to Janice Julian for overseeing the production of the audio version of the book. Thank you sincerely, Dawn Hugh, for casting your expert eye on our back cover, and Donald Bennett, for standing in as our final proofreader. Finally, thank you, Alex Lee, for your professionalism and endless enthusiasm from start to finish.

Thank you, all.

AUTHOR'S NOTE

For the purpose of sharing some of the more important lessons learned along my journey, I have chosen to change the names and identifying details of certain individuals in this book, to protect their privacy.

March 22, 2012—Lehman Center for the Performing Arts, The Bronx, NY

"If hard work could kill you, I'd have been dead a long time ago."

Vincent

I HASTEN TO THE PODIUM STANDING BEFORE THE small group of college students. I know that the applause generated from fifty people—even if enthusiastic—will only last so long. I grab the few seconds in which to perch my glasses on my nose, and open flat my two pages of notes. Before me sits a group of business students, ready to learn some tips and pointers from my experience as an entrepreneur.

This is not my first speech, so I'm not nervous. I understand, like anything else in life and in business, that as long as you add thought and care, you will deliver a quality product worthy of an audience's attention or, in the case of my line of business, consumption.

I also know that brevity is king. It is never OK to take for granted the time and effort others give you. Just as no one has to patronize your restaurant, or wait in line to buy your product, no one has to listen to you drone on. I learned that lesson at one of my first speaking engagements. I had prepared an epistle. I went on and on, my head buried in my notes. Eventually, the poor emcee had to tap me on my shoulder and whisper—red-faced—that I really had to wrap it up. As I have never considered myself too old or too successful to grow, I absorbed that lesson like a damp sponge. No one will need to tap on my shoulder today. "I hope my business experience will inspire you," I begin.

I'm particularly excited about addressing this audience because they're here by choice, eager for some kind of "map" with which to chart their adventure as the next generation of enterprise builders. Young, energetic, and wide-eyed, they're standing at a pivotal stage of their lives. I'm older—admittedly a little slower now—but no less giddy about seizing opportunities to build something wonderful.

It sounds too obvious to mention, but a college education gives them an advantage. A man like me appreciates a growth milestone like this. I grew up "country poor" with only a couple years of high school under the single belt I owned. These students are, in my opinion, going about it the right way. They're training their minds before building their business muscle. By the time I completed *my* highest degree—my GED—I was a thirty-six-year-old milkman. But, at the same time, I look out at the faces before me and wonder if this set of eager and educated minds will have that all-important fire in the belly. It is not something that can be handed to you. The best self-motivation is the kind that's self-generated.

I go through my talking points, taking time to cover the basic tenets: quality products and service, hard work, smart work, and the importance of perseverance. To help make it real in their minds, I include a few personal examples. Some are strictly business-related, while others fall under the category of universal life advice. I deliver one in particular with a slight tone of urgency, as it can either cement or crack the foundation of a person's future. It is this: "Do not spend more than you make." I repeat this simple rule to anyone with ears.

I end my presentation in the allotted time, wishing I could completely peel back the curtains and share the human side of my journey. I'd like to tell these kids that obstacles exist only in the minds of the uninspired. I grew up so poor that my family's tiny home—shop included—could have easily fit into what is today my company's staff lunchroom. I'd like to share some of my personal philosophies and hard-earned lessons. Without those cornerstones, I would have crumbled a long time ago. I also want to share something about spirituality. Life can level you unconscious sometimes. The only net that kept me from freefalling into despair was my faith. Today there is not enough time, however, and so I smile as I wrap up and wish the young warriors every success.

I have spent much of my life fielding questions from would-be entrepreneurs. Inevitably, I'd pull examples from my own archives: the harrowing crossroads, the unexpected potholes, the missed turnoffs, and the sacrifices demanded by such a journey. The satisfaction I get from seeing our conversations translated into results is beyond description. I know the adrenaline rush they feel when risk, sacrifice, and hard work are eventually rewarded. This is especially true in an age when instant gratification has practically reached "app" status.

While I have never grown tired of telling these stories— and doubt I ever will—it never occurred to this high-school dropout that I should share my experience in a book. That idea came from my wonderful children. *Before you forget, Dad.* At first I laughed at the thought. After a while, however, I realized that they were right. And so, on the morning of my seventy-fourth birthday, I sat at my dining table, and began committing to paper the first set of notes to this book.

Like my products, I mean to use only the best ingredients for my readers, including generous heaps of personal anecdotes, moderate dashes of practical examples, and a hint of personal philosophy. The arena of life is both scary and exhilarating. It takes courage to not only show up, but to stay and battle all that will come your way. You will face the naysayers, the takers, and opponents who fight dirty. You will face your share of mistakes, anxiety, and failure. No one gets it right all the time. At the other end of the spectrum, you will encounter the extended hands, the helpful words of advice, and the unexpected allies. Then, at some point, you will look up, wipe away the sweat, see your rewards before you, and wonder why you wasted time stuck in fear.

I hope that this book fuels you with the encouragement and energy to push forward. If something within these pages leaves you with the robust aftertaste of confidence and inspiration, then I will have done my job. Let no one fool you—business is a gamble. We'd all be billionaires if we each had a crystal ball. The only way to move up is to take a chance. That's the beauty of living in America, though. If you're prepared to roll up your sleeves and really give it your all, you can make that dream of yours come true.

PART ONE

The apprenticeship years

CHAPTER 1

First strokes on a clean canvas

"I live in gratitude for the hard life that came with my humble beginnings. It might have taken me longer to grasp certain lessons had it not been for the benefit of that particular petri dish. It's what ignited in me the fire to make something of myself."

Vincent

WHEN I WAS BORN IN AUGUST OF 1940, WORLD WAR II was well underway, engineers were already working on color television, and Mount Rushmore was just a year away from being unveiled. I say this, not to give a history lesson, but to marvel at how tiny and far-removed my birthplace and home-town of Springfield, Jamaica, was from the world.

Tucked away in the remote, shady hills eleven miles above Montego Bay, Springfield had no electricity, no running water, not even a paved road. The only things that came close to scraping the sky were the magnificent breadfruit and pimento trees. Encouraged by seasonal rainfall and mineral-rich soil, they stretched high and wide. In many ways it was still a privilege to live there. On a clear day, you could almost see the island's northern coastline brimming under the brilliant sunshine.

Ours was basically the only Chinese family in Springfield. We were, at least for a while, a family of ten children: Yuklin, Que, Mae, Thompson, King, Nuke, Ilene, me, George, and Winston. For a short time there was another Chinese family—the Wongs—with a small shop in nearby Kensington, about a mile from Springfield. Our tiny setups were typical of the kind found in that era across the island—impossibly crammed yet fairly impressive in its range of goods. From flour to fabric, the Chinese store was your one-stop shop. That was a good thing. If you lived in the countryside, it was usually your only shop.

Looking like a New York general store's much poorer cousin, our shop sold everything from sugar, flour and fish, to rope, hammer and nails, and even repair supplies for the village cobbler. Most among the first waves of Chinese settlers in the island chose the grocer's shop as their livelihood, even if they once held professions in their native China. I suppose that in those pioneering days of colonial Jamaica, integrating and surviving came first. Owning and running a shop was no doubt the easiest way for the non-English-speaking newcomers to achieve both. Little wonder then that there was not a corner of the island's landscape that didn't have its resident Chinese shop.

My parents, Henry and Nukelyn HoSang, worked their general store fourteen hours a day, six days a week, while bringing their large family into the world. Two would not make it to adulthood—Ilene, the youngest girl, would pass away before her third birthday after contracting mumps. My older brother King and I would end up being the ones to claim her body at the hospital in Montego Bay. I was eight at the time. Thompson, the brother before King, would also pass away in childhood from a congenital heart defect.

As was typical then of Chinese shop families, work and home shared the same roof. Our house was a basic structure: wood walls and floor perched on concrete columns raised slightly off the mineral-rich red earth, with a zinc roof on top. Inside, the basic wood ceiling offered something of a buffer. When it rained, the fat raindrops pummeled hard at the zinc sheet, producing the sound of a hundred drums out of sync. And, in the true spirit of making the most of every square inch of precious real estate, the gap under the house became the natural nesting place for the hens and ducks. Being one of the smaller boys, it was my duty to collect their eggs.

Our dwelling had four rooms: the first front room was for the shop itself, while the second was for the requisite rum bar. The two in the rear served as our bedrooms. A thin piece of wood acted as the "wall" that separated the shop from the bedrooms. The sleeping arrangement was a practical one—the girls huddled with our mom, the boys with our father. That's how it was then when space was scarce—your parents didn't sleep in the same room. That would have been a luxury. Of course, the single wooden outhouse served us all. But not even a house this basic were we in a position to own. We were tenants.

My earliest memory places me in our shop at the age of six or seven. To this day I can still smell the cod that had been delivered that morning. That sharp smell of salted fish never really leaves your nostrils. I remember looking out from behind the counter with my oldest sister, Yuklin. As there was no television or telephone, our entertainment came in Sunday walks, making crude toys out of sticks, or helping with the shop when we were asked to. Our parents never really forced us to help, so when they did ask, we generally obeyed them. That day, Yuklin was busy crocheting in a chair, when a customer came in and bid us good morning. "Vincent," my sister nudged. "Please help the lady." I greeted the customer with the standard *good morning, ma'am*, and asked what I could get for her. She needed a nice piece of pickled mackerel, she said.

I walked over to where the mackerel barrel sat, and paused. The only way to get the fish was to reach in and pull it out. I immediately saw my challenge. I was barely a head taller than the container. Somehow I had to get my arm in there. After a few seconds studying the situation, I shimmied up with a little jump, and hoisted myself onto the thin lip of the barrel. Balancing on my stomach, I steadied myself with one hand on the other side of the barrel, and reached into the brine with my free hand. Seconds later, I proudly produced a wet, fat, shiny fish, weighed it for the lady, wrapped it in newsprint paper, collected the money, and made change.

That may have been my first memory, but I have proof that my working career began even earlier. The proof is a two-inch scar on my left forearm.

According to my parents, I was taking empty soda bottles to the crate, one by one, when I tripped and landed on one of the bottles, breaking it into pieces. One piece tore into my arm. There was no doctor in Springfield, so I didn't get stitches. The village midwife—the same one who delivered us all—cleaned the deep cut, which eventually healed.

Every now and then I glance at the mark that grew with me. Somewhat faded but still visible, it has a way of transporting me down a rabbit hole back to another time. I'm glad I bear a permanent reminder of my shop life with my family in our country home. It's the one thing I don't ever want to forget: the lessons learned from a life of little.

My father had arrived on the island from South China in the 1920s, several years ahead of my mother so as to get settled first. Born in 1885, he was considerably older than she was. Both were Hakka Chinese, a people known for their nomadic history and pioneering spirit. By the time Henry brought his bride over from China he was already forty, which might explain why they had us in rapid succession. By the time I came along, he was almost fifty-five.

We were not my father's first family, however. Before my mother's arrival to the island, he fathered three sons (Leo, Morrel, and Dorrel) with two Jamaican women. As children, we would only see our half-brothers a handful of times, but not because of any family drama. In those days, having other families was not an uncommon occurrence among the first waves of male Chinese settlers, particularly for those who arrived without their wives.

As for the reason my father chose to settle in Springfield, I can only assume that it had to do with its lack of competition. There he could be "king of his own hill," so to speak. While his reasoning held merit, however, Springfield had issues. With no industry through which to employ the villagers—his customers—there was little disposable income. The only time money flowed was when generous overseas relatives mailed the occasional money order from America or England. As the only wiring service we had was the telegram, most had no choice but to wait for those precious envelopes. Otherwise, Springfield's residents generally lived off the earth, and survived on the bartering system. Instead of their cash for our sugar, they'd offer us a head of cabbage, fresh eggs, or fruit—things we already had, things we could not use to pay our rent.

My mother did not like shop life. Her body language said it all. She rarely smiled at our customers and made little attempt at general pleasantries. In her defense, she was probably plain exhausted from raising us kids and tending to the shop from daybreak to sunset. Ten minutes in a chair with a cup of tea would have been the only downtime she knew—not ideal for someone with advanced diabetes. I can only assume she used ice to keep her insulin cool since we had no refrigeration. Then there was the added frustration of facing customer after customer trying to pay us in kind. It broke my heart to watch her do something every day that gave her no joy, nor the means with which to buy some comfort.

My poor father never gave up, nor did he vent his frustrations on us kids. In fact, I don't remember a single time he raised his voice at us. Desperate to make things work, he tried his hand at rearing pigs for slaughter, and running a basic bakery in a tiny shack next to the shop. His dough mixer was a simple wooden trough. The only thing that resembled a machine was a dough breaker—a manual one, of course—that required the dough to be pushed through the roller at one end, then back through the second roller at the other end until the dough was ready. He did this, day after day, for customers who couldn't even pay for the bread. One day, the top of the brick oven caved in. My father walked away from the rubble, and never baked again.

Even as he struggled, my father continued helping his customers. He simply didn't have the heart to say no. Sometimes he'd give the goods away and make a note in his little credit book, knowing full well that payment would never come. *Mas',*

Henry, the customer would say, *I have no dinner for my family tonight*. With a nod and whisper of a sigh, he'd pick up a piece of dried cod, wrap it in paper, and hand it over in silence.

My grasp of how important it was to make ends meet took root when I was about ten. I was in the shop, this time with my father, when one of our suppliers walked in. Mr. Greaves was a white Jamaican man, tall, slim, and a little on the hairy side. He had traveled from Kingston to repossess some of the fabric he had delivered to my father a few weeks before. The exchange between the two was quiet—almost sad. I could tell that Mr. Greaves did not wish to be there. As he handed my father the receipt for the returned merchandise, my father apologized for being unable to pay, his face hanging low. I felt a sudden heaviness in my stomach. I would have done anything to find that money for my father. I wanted to see him lift his eyes again.

We never made money, not even when the Wongs—our only real competition in the neighboring town—packed it up early in the game, gave us their two dogs, and left for better prospects. Their departure and our continued struggle should have signaled to my father that it was time to seek our livelihood elsewhere too, but, with so many kids in tow, he was not nearly as nimble.

We stayed, continuing to live on the bare minimum—and I mean *minimum*. We each had just one or two changes of clothes. That worked out fine because there was no closet in the house anyway. Our "closet" was a set of nails driven into the bedroom walls. We each had a single pair of shoes, which we saved for school and church. Therefore, unless you were sitting before your teacher or Jesus, you generally went around barefoot. Needless to say, our feet were perpetually copper-colored from the rich red soil. If you outgrew your pair or ruined it, you pretty much went without until your next hand-me-down. Once, when I had worn out my pair, I had to temporarily share patent leather shoes with my older sister Nuke.

We didn't even own toothbrushes. Instead, we rinsed our gums with water and gnawed at raw sugarcane stalks, allowing the rough straw-like strings to run between our teeth. The sugarcane floss did not fail us, I'm happy to say. My dentist will confirm that I still have most of my own teeth.

One thing we never wanted for was food. It was the Chinese way—food and shelter above all else. We ate simply but regularly, living off our father's garden where he grew his favorite Chinese vegetables, like bitter melon, *bok choy*, and mustard. From our yard we enjoyed poultry, pork, and goat meat. Friday was usually red meat day. That's when one of the villagers would slaughter a cow, which meant that Springfield's residents could enjoy a little treat. On those days we splurged on steak, with Mom also taking the cheaper stomach parts to make soup.

My parents rarely spoke of their lives in China. Their English was functional, so I can't claim there was a language barrier. We just never thought to ask. All they ever volunteered was that Mom had made the journey on a boat with live animals for food, and that Dad had been a bookkeeper for his fishmonger father.

Our father was as easy-going and mild-mannered with us as he was with his customers. Our mother was the disciplinarian who made sure we didn't fall in harm's way. She was the one who marched us off to our baths, made sure we were in our bed at a respectable time, and set chores for us. I was in charge of cleaning all the lampshades on the hurricane lamps. We only owned a grand total of three, but I remember deciding that it was an important job because soot built up on the glass coverings every night. The only way we were going to get light from them was if I cleaned them. Carefully, and with great pride, I'd gather some old newspaper, dampen it with water, and gently rub away at the soot. I did this every day after school.

When I wasn't doing chores, homework, or hanging out in the shop, I'd sometimes go for walks, not daring to go too far. My mother was not the kind of woman whose patience you tested. My older brothers were more adventurous, but I didn't relish getting into trouble. I had seen them suffer the consequences. Mom was swift at converting her feather duster into a small whip, or using a leather strap to tie us to the foot of the bed. She had other tricks too. Once, when King had been particularly naughty, she confiscated his favorite dinner bowl. I guess she knew he'd feel that more than the sting of a whip.

Occasionally I'd pass the time away by accompanying our helper, Miss Katie, to the river where she washed our clothes. Her task was brutal. She'd trek a mile over a hill, also barefoot, with the basket of clothes balanced on her head, wash each piece by hand, then walk back with the same load, now wet and significantly heavier. She sang the entire time, but not with the joy that usually comes with singing aloud. The words were drawn out, and her gaze always cast to the ground. I did my best to help her, but the most I could do was carry a few pieces. Even as a young child, I was unhappy knowing that someone had to work that hard for so little.

That even a family as poor as ours could afford a helper reflected the third-world reality around us. It dictated that labor—particularly the unskilled kind—could be had at bargain-basement prices. The sad part was that she was one of the lucky ones. She had a job. We had two helpers, in fact. Miss Katie was a "live-in." Her "room" was really a corner, a tiny matchbox area that sat next to the kitchen. Her "mattress" was a large piece of cloth stuffed with banana leaves or coconut coir. The other helper, whom my mother nicknamed Moonshine, was younger and lived just down the road from us.

Weekdays meant school for us kids. The village elementary school sat a mile's walk away, which meant you had to run at a nice clip if you wanted to go home for lunch and return before the bell rang for the afternoon session. The single-room school took its students to grade six only, which meant that you had to leave Springfield for high school. Our classroom was pretty simple. The chairs and tables didn't match, and the blackboard went unused when we ran out of chalk. Sometimes, if it was a nice day out or a group needed to focus on a lesson in a quiet place, the teachers would hold their class under the cool canopy of a large tree. One teacher happened to be our landlord's wife. A stickler for discipline, she stuttered at the first sign of misbehavior. To her credit, it took a whole lot of misbehaving on our part for her to grab her trusty leather strap.

Saturdays was our "busy" day at the shop. I'd be there most of the time to help, even though we rarely saw more than a trickle of customers. We were officially closed on Sundays, but only because the law required it. Sundays meant rest, family time, and church.

It was in Springfield that I was first introduced to the good Lord. I have to admit that, while I liked attending school, I didn't feel the same enthusiasm about going to church. It wasn't that I didn't enjoy learning about God. If you were raised on that island—particularly in the countryside—you pretty much grew up with religion. It was the need to sit still for so long that didn't sit well with me. Stillness at that age drove me a little crazy. So, when the spirit moved me, I'd skip church. That went on until one of the villagers, an old-timer, saw me one Sunday morning playing outside the shop with a toy truck. "Truck" might have been a bit of a stretch considering that I had made it without the benefit of actual tools, but in my mind it was the finest toy ever. Dressed in his Sunday suit along with hat and cane, the old man frowned as he drew close. "No, no, this won't do," he said to my father with a wink. "This young chap needs to find himself in church!" There ended my day off from the pew.

My father took no offence at the gentleman's prodding. It was perfectly acceptable then for the villagers to raise its children as one. The occasional exchange of parental duties was also common. Such was the case in the relationship we had with Miss Camelita, or "Miss Cami" as we called her, who lived a few minutes away from us. She had become a single mother to her four children years before, when her Chinese common-law husband, a distant cousin of ours, left for Montego Bay. After little success at his own shop, he decided to try his fortune in town instead. His departure meant his family struggled. To help Miss Cami, most Saturday evenings we cooked enough dinner for both families to share.

Our two families enjoyed a natural exchange of kindness. Miss Cami, recognizing that my mother's limited English made her uncomfortable outside of the shop and home, ran the occasional errand for my mother in Montego Bay. When I spent two weeks in the hospital recovering from an appendectomy, it was Miss Cami who stayed in Montego Bay to feed me while I recuperated. Every day she walked to the hospital with a hot home-cooked meal. Meanwhile, back in Springfield, my mother watched over Miss Cami's children. These gestures and acts of compassion were a big part of my youth. I consider myself blessed for having lived during such gentler times.

It wasn't always utopia, of course. From time to time we were teased for our differences—how we looked, how we ate, and how we sounded, and there were a few who expressed their curiosity about us with some degree of crassness. Those individuals we took as the exception to the rule, however, and no one was physically cruel. We therefore assumed our role as the village minority with the same tolerance and grace extended to us by the majority.

While life was basic for us, we did enjoy the occasional treat. Our lucky break came when our oldest sister, Yuklin, left to work with another Chinese family in Montego Bay. The Kelly Wongs had a successful supermarket, which meant that Yuklin had a good job. It also meant that every Christmas she'd come through our front door with her arms full—one store-bought toy for each of us. That would be our gift quota for the year, birthdays included. We weren't miserable over it, though, and we never complained to our parents, even though there were times we couldn't help but secretly long for better. I know I did.

What our parents couldn't give us in our hands they gave in abundance in our hearts—self-love and confidence. My father always smiled with all his teeth when I reminded him that I wanted to become a doctor. Looking back, I realize how remarkable that was. It showed how much faith he had, not just in my capabilities, but in the universe. There he was, a man who could barely pay his bills, welcoming his son's vision with an open heart. His willingness to let me dream in spite of our situation went far beyond a father loving his child unconditionally.

His act of faith sent up a protective shield around me at a critical stage of my life. It made me obstacle-blind. It let me believe in a future that was grossly inconsistent with my circumstances.

It was a gift beyond measure.

Our mom did her part by showering us with physical affection. She constantly fussed over us, never letting us forget that we were special. "Come and kiss your mom," she'd often say as she smiled and grabbed me with another endless squeeze. My mother loved her children with a passion that crossed even earthly boundaries. I know she saw Thompson's death before it came. Her premonition happened the day before he passed. It was a Saturday night, and we were all helping our father entertain an aunt who was visiting. Mom was lying on her bed, unable to stand a minute longer after an exhausting day. Suddenly, over the chatter, we heard her knocking urgently on the thin partition. Mae and I ran to her. Sitting up, she stared ahead in the direction of the other bedroom. "Vincen'!" she said, her eyes widening. "Vincen', who insigh' odda room?"

When we looked, however, we saw no one. Our mother would not calm down. She kept insisting that she had seen the shadow of a child sitting on the bed. After a while, we got her to close her eyes.

The next day was Sunday. We were all taking our time to get up, when we heard a frantic knock at the gate. It was one of our customers, pleading with us to open the shop. Her daughter had a fever so she needed white overproof rum to bring it down. My father nodded right away and signaled to me to help the customer while he rested. I didn't hesitate. The circles under his eyes were deep with fatigue.

At the time we had a pet dog, Lion. He was, as his name suggests, a large canine. That morning, he happened to be sleeping in the shop. The second I opened the door for the customer, Lion leapt up in a rage, flew over the counter, and bolted out into the street. My brother Thompson ran past me, calling after Lion. Seconds later Thompson collapsed like a ragdoll. His weak heart, the reason behind his sickly childhood, had finally quit on him. By the time we carried him inside the house and laid him on his bed—the same bed on which our mother had seen the shadow—he was gone.

There would be other incidents that made me aware of this strange connection to "knowing." One of my own happened while we were still in Springfield. The occasion was a fun day at a nearby park, to commemorate a national holiday. As part of the festivities, the officials decided to hold a raffle for a beautiful bedroom vanity. Just as the announcer was about to pull the winning number out of the box, a voice spoke in my head: *Your sister is going to win.* It came as suddenly as a small gust of wind on a calm day. Sure enough, Mae won. She smiled for a week straight.

So there were struggles—sadness too. Through it all, however, we always looked for a reason to smile and find real happiness in our simple lives. As for our poverty, it never quite dawned on me how poor we really were. Then again, I had rarely set foot out of Springfield. Other than a couple textbooks with some pictures and a handful of journeys into Montego Bay, I had encountered no other reference point that opened my eyes or offered a new perspective.

That all changed the day I got my first glimpse of America.

CHAPTER 2

A peek into the future

"If I had to single out one truism, it would be this:
Attitude, not aptitude, determines altitude. I first
came across the famous Zig Ziglar saying decades
ago in a fortune cookie. Since then, I've kept it in
my wallet and in my mind."

Vincent

I WAS ABOUT NINE YEARS OLD WHEN I NOTICED
that some of the villagers would disappear for a few months,
only to return looking like anything but ordinary country
dwellers. These were farm workers—contract workers who
went to America to harvest sugarcane. I saw their transforma-
tion the moment they returned. Decked out in store-bought

clothes, they'd flock to our rum bar to entertain the crowd with animated stories of life in America, which meant a much-needed windfall for our family each time they came home. For me, however, it was all about the show and tell.

The crowd would linger for hours to see some of the incredible things they had bought in America. Everyone ran their own commentary as the returning residents displayed item after item. Every gem caught my eye—marbles that were bigger, fancier, and shinier than anything I'd ever seen; perfectly smooth lead pencils with huge, rubbery erasers that looked good enough to eat. I swore to myself that if I ever had the chance to own one of those pencils, I'd never use it. I'd keep it forever. One of my schoolmates got a ladies bicycle with hub brakes. Even though the bicycle was secondhand and gender-incorrect, none of us cared. To us, he was the luckiest kid in Springfield.

As the evening progressed, the travelers would regale the crowd with stories that produced roars of laughter and shouts of praise. They also indulged in antics designed to flash their fortune, like "accidentally" dropping an American coin on the ground, then lighting a five-shilling bill like a small torch to go searching for the "lost" change. I remember gasping at the sight of the precious money melting into ashes, my mouth open and eyes bulging. Of all the amazing treasures the farm workers brought back, however, none caught my attention quite like Mr. Leach's souvenir. With the money he had earned sweating in a cane field, Mr. Leach bought a car.

I will never forget the moment I saw it. That Dodge sat there like a young bull—strong, self-assured, and powerful. Gleaming from a fresh wax job, its sturdy body easily dwarfed Springfield's feeble shacks and narrow, crooked roads. I held my breath as the neurons fired in my head. *You can go to America, work hard, and buy a car, Vinnie. An actual car! Not even your father has one, and he's the big man in town!*

I had always heard about America, of course. Who hadn't? Until that day, however, it was more fantasy than fact. For me, it was just the name of another country. That all changed the moment I saw the Dodge. From then on, America was a real place. America was reward for hard work. It was beautiful cars, incredible marbles, and the most amazing school supplies a kid ever saw. That day, I planted the first seed of my future. *When I grow up,* I said to myself, *I'm going to America.*

When I turned twelve, life as I knew it came to an abrupt end. We had failed to improve our situation. Bankrupt and unable to pay his bills, my father sold the business for a song. That, however, was not the worst of it.

I still remember the defeat in his eyes as he quietly told us that we were all going to live in separate homes. He had made arrangements with distant relatives in other towns across the island, he said. The list included a cousin whom he had twice helped years before with loans for a shop. Now, Henry HoSang had no choice but to call in the favor. He told us where each child would be going as if handing out deployment details. It wasn't that he did this without feeling. He did this knowing he had no choice.

I was lucky. Only three of us would stay with our parents: my older sister Nuke, youngest brother, Winston, who was just a baby then, and me. We five were to relocate to Montego Bay. Mae and Que would go to Kingston. George would live with distant relatives in a rural town called Anchovy. King, the brother to whom I was closest, was already in Montego Bay attending high school and boarding with some family friends.

We did not ask our father a single question, not even the one burning question any child would have: *But when will we see you again?* It was not our place to challenge him. This golden rule lived beyond the walls of our home. In those days, adults in general did not readily entertain conversations with children. Only an insolent child dared to speak uninvited. As we stood there, receiving the most devastating news of our young lives, our father heard no protests from us. I told myself that we would all be OK. God would watch over us all.

Our mother sobbed the entire time. "You give away kittens and puppies, not children," she wailed to my father. But Henry HoSang did not cry, at least, not in front of his family. I can only guess at the agony he felt. Starting over again was highly unlikely. At almost seventy, he had nothing to his name. In all his years of trying to build a business and feed his large family, he had not managed to acquire property. Such a safety net might have made the difference, but he had done the best he could then, just as he was doing now.

My siblings and I took his lead. We squeezed our lips together, blinked back the tears, and remained silent. We didn't even huddle to talk. That was the last night my parents would ever see us all together.

Montego Bay was a blustery sauna the day we arrived. I remember wanting to strip off the cotton shirt that had pasted itself to my back. When we got to our first stop, a narrow two-story building owned by a Mr. Chin Fatt, I wiped the sweat off my face with my forearm. The two-room flat above the shop was our new home. I soon found reason to smile, however. It was going to be a sardine-can squeeze, but King was going to move in with us.

The school year was still in session, so we wasted no time getting settled in. With our new school only a half hour's walk up the adjacent hill, I quickly learned the new route and watched over my sister, making sure she didn't get too close to the road. We were not used to traffic.

With our new life came a new job for me. Every day, my father gave me ten pence to buy a loaf of bread for the family. It came with the strict instructions to be careful with the money. "Come home with the bread, Vincen," my father would say gently as he pressed the money into my palm. "Don't forget, son." Each time he did this, I could sense the words he did not say: *It's all we have.* No longer did I see my father's eyes crinkle in a smile. They had lost their shine.

Within a couple weeks, the new living arrangements changed. Again our father delivered the news plain and straight. They were sending Nuke to live with the same relatives in Anchovy that had taken George in. The biggest change came for King, who was now sixteen. As my father could no longer afford his school fees, King would be leaving school and moving to a town called Christiana, where an aunt of ours owned a wholesale shop and bakery. The plan was for him to work for her, and make his start in life. The move to Christiana ended up being the right one. A cousin found King an even better job with one of the bauxite companies in the area. Snagging an entry-level position in such a thriving sector meant the start of a bright future for my brother.

Then there was me. I was to stay in Montego Bay, also with a distant relative. I learned about this while getting dressed for school one morning. I was buttoning my khaki shirt, when my father came up to me. "Vincen," he said softly. "Vincen,' you go to live with new uncle now. Go pack your bag."

I hardly paused before doing as I was told. He gave no explanation, of course, but he didn't have to. I knew his financial situation had worsened. I packed my small bag in less than five minutes before going to my mom. She had been complaining of feeling unwell, so I walked over to where she was sitting and gave her a hug. When she returned a feeble pat, I knew something was wrong. I gave her a worried look as Dad rubbed his hand over my head. "Be good, Vincen'. Be helpful boy to your uncle."

I nodded. I told myself that I was still lucky—at least my parents were in the same town. He and Mom were now left with just one child in their care, Winston.

I would learn only decades later that my father, desperate to earn an income of some kind, had turned to gambling at this point. It was not something I had ever known him to indulge in. He did not do the actual gambling, apparently, but had someone else stand in for him. Eventually he would lose just about everything, including his children.

That morning, it took me twenty minutes to walk to the house and shop of Harrison Ho. I was relieved when I stopped in front of the two-story structure bearing his address. This uncle was one of the lucky ones who lived above the shop, and not behind it. At thirty-six, he was my father's much younger cousin, with roots in the same ancestral village in China. The only thing we knew about him, other than the village connection, was that he lived alone.

When I got to his place that morning, I was racing against the school bell. With one ear listening out for its loud ring, sure to be any second, I gave a quick "hello" to my uncle, nodded shyly to the petite Chinese lady behind the counter with the curious smile, handed over my suitcase, and dashed off. That afternoon when I returned from school, I found my uncle in the shop.

"You know wha' to call me?" he said with a tone so flat, I wasn't sure if it was a question or statement.

"No, sir," I said, my eyes on the floor.

"You call me *Ahshook*."

"Yes, Ahshook."

"Go now. Aunt Sylvia show you room."

"Yes, Ahshook."

The Chinese word, which means *my father's youngest brother*, was a bit of a misnomer in this situation, but it at least reminded me that I was still with family. The short conversation was the extent of our interaction that day.

Smiling, her head slightly tilted, Sylvia beckoned with her hand as she made her way to the stairs. When we got to my room, she said softly that I should pay a visit to the tailor the next day. I needed some more things, she said. One change of clothes would not do. Then she excused herself and disappeared down the stairs so I could settle in. I thought that Uncle was awfully lucky to have such a kind worker.

As the echoes of her last steps evaporated into the late afternoon air, it occurred to me that I had never stayed in another person's house before, at least not without my parents. The thought brought on a sudden heaviness in my stomach, and small lump in my throat. I longed to see a familiar face. I wondered how my siblings were and whether they were with nice families.

I stood there, chin on my chest, and stared at the wood planks beneath my feet. After a few minutes, feeling no better, I lifted my head and scanned my room. There was a narrow bed to one side, with a small window next to it. Even though it was wide open, there was a slight mustiness in the air—a familiar smell. I soon realized that it was coming from the desk that sat against the other wall. My new "desk" was actually two salted-codfish crates turned upside down and pushed together. It was the scent of our Springfield shop.

I thought it was nice of my uncle to have thought of a desk for my homework. Before that, my only desk had been my lap. On closer inspection, I saw yet another surprise waiting for me on the bed—a toothbrush. I smiled. For the first time in my life I had my own bed, my own room, *and* a toothbrush. Maybe, I thought to myself, maybe everything would be OK after all.

I didn't have the words to describe it then, but at that moment I decided that I was lucky. I somehow understood that I could miss my family and still be happy. In some ways I was already better off. This uncle had a real flush toilet.

Weeks barely passed before the restless trade winds blew through our family once more. My mother, who had been complaining of feeling weak and breathless, was diagnosed with tuberculosis. We were not allowed to get near her to say goodbye the day she left for the Chinese sanatorium in Kingston. All

I could do was stand and watch as the train pulled away with the only mother I'd ever known, the same mother who had wiped my nose, nursed my colds, and shooed me off to bed since the day I was born. She waved anxiously through the window, her eyes swollen and red. It would be several years before I'd see her again.

My mother's departure was not the end of our family shuffle, however. Not long after, my father announced that he had found a job with a Chinese family in a town called Claremont, located several hours away. The family had a wholesale business and needed the help. Dad would take Winston with him. By the time my father told me all this, he had already packed his bags.

We were seeds scattered to the wind. Now I was truly on my own.

CHAPTER 3

Teachers of different kinds

"There were many times in my life when things seemed to be going wrong for me. I have no doubt that it was God at work. He was forcing my hand so I'd make certain choices."

Vincent

IF LIFE WAS SLOW IN SPRINGFIELD, IT DID AN about-turn once I went to live in Montego Bay. Each morning, I'd get up at six, help Uncle in the shop for a half hour before Sylvia arrived, and then go to school. After school, I'd head straight home instead of playing games with the other kids. By the time I arrived at four for my second shift, Sylvia, whom I addressed as "Aunt Sylvia," would be behind the counter greeting me with a smile. Uncle, meanwhile, would either be napping or seeing his vendors in town.

My shop duties were simple. I'd take the bulk items and wrap them in smaller portions in paper funnels, pack the shelves, make popsicles, and help Aunt Sylvia serve the customers and make change. When credit customers came in, I'd carefully make the entry in Uncle's book reserved for those transactions, and always checked for accuracy.

A hard-working lady, Aunt Sylvia's duties extended to the kitchen as our daily cook. In the evenings, the three of us would take turns eating dinner at the kitchen table. While one ate, the others served the customers. On Sundays she helped us with all the cleaning and preparation chores for the following week. My Sunday duties included cleaning the refrigerator, repacking it, and making syrup-flavored ice cubes aptly called Suck Sucks.

Even though Uncle Harrison was all about customer service, he did not seem to like people. I knew this, not just from his short interactions with me, but also from his rough demeanor with everyone else, including his customers. I was convinced his mouth didn't know how to form a smile. The only person he seemed to tolerate was Aunt Sylvia. I often wondered what a sunnier approach might have done for his business, which seemed to be doing well despite his gruff exterior. My father's shop was nothing like this. In Uncle's shop, just about everything sold. Here, just about every customer paid with real money. For that alone I felt Uncle Harrison could have smiled at least once a week.

Even though this was not my family's business, I began to watch the dynamics in Uncle's shop. I observed how quickly certain items sold. I noticed his attempts at offering customers goods other than groceries—like pots, plates, and cutlery. If something wasn't moving, he stopped selling it. If something sparked, he added a little more initially, and then a lot more if the numbers looked good. It was a constant course adjustment. I took note of it all. *So this is how it's supposed to be*, I said to myself. I had to admit, it gave me a small rush.

Once we closed at eight, Aunt Sylvia would immediately prepare a warm bath for me. The gesture, itself filled with warmth, took time to complete, as she first had to boil the water before pouring it into the zinc tub. Once dry and in my nightclothes, I'd spend the next hour or two doing homework. That was perhaps the hardest part of the day. By then I was so drained, all I could think of was crawling into my bed and pulling the thin cotton sheet over me. I always got my work done regardless of how tired I was, but my enthusiasm depended on the subject. For math, I'd plough through. For something that required a whole lot of reading, I'd drag it out. Despite my best efforts to stay on top of my studies, however, my grades fell. Whether they suffered because I was at a more challenging school, or because I had less time to study, I'll never know. I can at least say that I remained a happy schoolboy, thanks in part to schoolmates who made me feel welcome, and who saw to it that I did not neglect the kid in me:

"Vinnie was the new kid at Ms. Meylers' Preparatory School. All we knew about his home life was that he was living with a guardian uncle who seemed to treat him well enough. We never heard Vinnie complain, at any rate. He rarely talked about his family, but always mentioned if he'd received a letter, or some kind of communication from them. That's when his eyes would all but disappear behind his smile.

"When we became good friends, he'd stop by my house on his way to school so we could finish the short walk together. At school he was one of the quieter boys who actually did his work. But, oh, he had a sense of humor all right. He delivered with stealth.

"Otherwise, Vinnie was like any other boy out there. During lunch break, he was always ready for a game of cricket or marbles, eager to raid a mango tree with us, and was generally on good terms with everyone. You didn't hear about him getting into fights or throwing a temper tantrum. He was a cool fellow.

"That said, there was this one time when we got ourselves in a sticky situation with some angry bees. It happened when Vin and I were attempting to extract a little honey from the beehive our headmistress kept at the back. In the end, all we got were some nasty stings after the bees chased us into the gap under the schoolroom. Fortunately, his stings weren't so bad that he was forced to tell his uncle about the escapade. I know he'd have been punished for it. The humiliation from being laughed at by the other kids was punishment enough.

"Even as a young boy, Vinnie took responsibility seriously. Every now and then some of us boys would pass by the shop to say hello or buy something. Sometimes he'd slip us a little treat of salted codfish at the far end of the counter. He was always jovial with the customers, and unfailingly polite. It was always, 'Good morning, sir, good morning, ma'am, how may I help you, thank you, and have a nice day.' Respect was the order of the day for him when he was behind that counter. It didn't seem scripted either. It was all quite natural.

"We continued our friendship when we graduated to the same high school, Cornwall College. On Sundays, the only day Vinnie had a half-day off, we'd spend a couple hours at the nearby beach swimming, jumping off rocks, or fishing. If we were lucky enough to snag a few fish, we'd take them back to my house, gut and clean our catch, and fry them whole. Once, we even caught an octopus with our bare hands and took that home too. Inevitably he'd announce at some point that he had to return to the shop to finish up some chores, but he didn't seem to mind. He never whined or complained about that. Not once.

"Vinnie learned as a boy what some learn only in adulthood: that with life comes duty. He just seemed comfortable with that rhythm of school and work, day in, day out. We couldn't have recognized it then because we were just kids, but for every minute he spent behind that counter, Vinnie was getting an education of a different kind."

Hollis "Barry" Levy
Retired Construction Manager

I had not given up on my wish to become a doctor, and continued to strain for the best grades I could get. I was not a star student—a steady one, yes, but those A's did not come without effort. Fortunately, I was blessed with teachers who not only knew their material, but who also seemed to enjoy their profession, with one exception. Mr. Atwell, while undeniably knowledgeable, made it clear to us that he did not intend to live his life teaching high school. In fact, he told his students that they should refrain from asking him questions of any kind.

The rumor was that he was saving his energy for his master's degree. One day, I did the unthinkable and raised my hand. I still can't remember what drove me to test him, but I ended up, along with some other brave classmates, in detention.

That afternoon I bent over the blank paper and began forming the words one after the other. Ten pages was our punishment. I used my neatest handwriting, as if bonus points would be given for good penmanship. A few minutes later into my work, I heard a hissing sound coming from my right. It was one of my fellow delinquents coming to my rescue. "Pssst! Vinnie!" he whispered. "Don't you need to get out of here? Not so small, man!" He pointed at his own exercise book. "Bigger letters!"

It felt a bit like cheating, but I figured it was worth a try. Thanks to my friend, I finished quickly. I don't know what explanation I gave my uncle that day, but it would have been one of the few times I was late for work. That day, I learned two things. From my friend I learned that sometimes you have to go for practicality. From my teacher—ironically—I learned that you should try to make your living from something you truly love.

Just as it's never good to burn your bridges, it's prudent to be kind and considerate to those you meet while building them. In my third year of high school, I had the privilege of being taught Spanish and English literature by a young and enthusiastic teacher:

"I remember Vincent for being a keen student: studious and disciplined. He was quiet—even bordering on shy—but friendly. Once you engaged him, however, it was obvious that he was comfortable in his own skin.

"Students express their skills and develop their capacities in their own way. Vincent would not have ranked in the top quarter performers, nor was he at the bottom. As a teacher, I appreciated him for his eagerness to learn. He was one of those students who applied themselves by listening. What he didn't understand he sought clarification on. There are a lot of students who don't perform in accordance to their potential. What made Vincent stand out was that he was one who was aware of his limitations, but prepared to give of his best. For that alone he was a model student.

"Neither his success nor humility as a grown man surprise me. I saw those qualities in him as a schoolboy. It was a matter of natural progression."

The Most Hon. P. J. Patterson, ON, OCC, PC, QC

Years later in New York, on separate occasions, I would reconnect with my old classmate and my former teacher. Both would be present at the official ground breaking of my Tappan plant. By then, Mr. Percival James Patterson had long graduated from standing before a classroom, to standing before a nation as Jamaica's sixth prime minister.

For a while I wasn't sure who was paying my school fees. Since we had split as a family, I had seen neither my parents nor my siblings, except for Yuklyn, who sometimes came to see me when she could. One day, my other sister, Nuke, appeared at the shop with money from my father. I knew then that he was at least paying some of my fees. I also learned that Nuke had gotten married. At only fifteen she was a young bride, even by that era's standards. Her husband, Ken Chin, immediately became a true brother to us. It was Ken who surprised me at the shop early one Sunday morning announcing that he was taking me to my mother in Kingston. She was better now but still recovering. I practically jumped when his small two-seater van pulled up. With space available only in the back, I used a wood box for a seat the whole way in.

Four hours later, after an exhausting drive over the island's mountainous roads, we approached the sanatorium in Kingston's downtown area. It was my first time in the capital city. I immediately liked the energy of it. There were more people, more buildings, and wider streets. Even the vehicles seemed to go by faster.

Minutes later I was with my mother. Instructed to keep a safe distance, we smiled and waved at each other, determined to make the most of the bittersweet moment. My mom locked her gaze on me, her eyes shining as she wiped away the few tears that escaped. I have never forgotten the kindness Ken showed me that day.

Seeing my mother made me miss her even more. I believe Aunt Sylvia sensed this. On my return, she hovered, always making eye contact with me, asking about my day, always asking whether I was hungry or needed something. If she was trying to make me feel comfortable, she succeeded. It was then that I began to suspect that her relationship with Uncle Harrison went beyond that of faithful employee. I suspected that she had won his heart. Little did she know that she had also won mine.

I'll never forget the day she asked me what I wanted for my birthday. The question lingered in the air. I had never been asked that before. My mouth went a little dry before I finally answered a few seconds later. "May I have…a belt, Aunt Sylvia?" I asked. "I don't have one." I stole a look at her while my chin went down. *Had I asked for too much?*

She nodded and smiled with a surprised look. "Yes, you're right. You don't have one, do you? Well, we'll just have to fix that." And so she got me my very own belt.

On the surface, my relationship with Uncle Harrison did not evolve. Always strict and generally silent, he found pleasure in only one thing—photography. Whatever free time he had was spent with that camera in his makeshift darkroom. Just as I thought I had him figured out, however, he'd do something to surprise me—like the time he shared some of his winnings after a night of mahjong. An avid gambler, he was never care-less like some who lost homes and businesses. He knew when to leave the table. The night he won, he gave me *soh-foot*, the Chinese name for a tip from one's winnings.

I took the lucky money and sent it to my mother the only way I could—through the mail. Naturally, I was too young to realize that sending cash in the mail was a gamble of a different kind. Fortunately, luck traveled with my small fortune, and my mom received the cash safely. A week later, Uncle asked me what I'd done with the money. When I told him, he said noth-ing, but I saw a sliver of a smile behind his poker face.

Then, when I was about fourteen, he surprised me with my first bicycle. I smiled so hard I thought for sure my cheeks would touch my eyes. I didn't care that it was a secondhand bicycle he'd bought from a lady customer. The photo taken of me posing with that gift, was also my first. I remember star-ing at it for the longest time with a smile that wouldn't end. It wasn't Uncle Harrison who took it, however, but Nuke and Ken. Uncle Harrison never pointed his camera at me once in the seven years I lived with him, but I didn't let that bother me. I had no expectations of him where affection was concerned. Today, the image of the shy boy with his first bicycle posing for his first photo sits in a frame in my office.

That bicycle and I became inseparable, even after I was almost mowed down by a driver. I don't think she even knew that she had sent a kid flying into the bushes. All I saw was the back of her head and the license plate, which I memorized.

Not only did the bicycle almost get me killed, it also got me a right reprimand from Uncle Harrison. I had come home one day from a ride to find the front door locked, as it usually was on a Sunday. In the seconds that followed, I must have temporarily lost my mind. Instead of knocking on the door, as I should have, I rang the bicycle bell a few times—loudly. Hearing it made me feel incredibly grown-up. When Uncle appeared at the door, he glared at me so hard I thought my face would peel off. "Oh! So you tassi drivah now, eh? Like to blow horn! Nes' time you knock like respectable person!"

The bicycle was, on closer inspection, an extremely generous gesture when you considered that a bicycle was also Uncle's only method of transportation at the time. In fact, he would not buy a car for several more years. I know that his choice to do without one was based on frugality. He could have afforded it. I saw what his sales were and knew of some of his expenses. Instead, he continued to build his padding, saving his reserves for his next investment. His discipline stood in sharp contrast to the many examples around us of others disrespecting their hard-earned money, and, by extension, themselves.

A case in point was a man from Montego Bay called Herman. Herman had also been one of those to travel abroad to seek his fortune. As the story went, he'd made a nice little nest egg for himself, which he proceeded to consume the moment he returned. The way I heard it from the locals, Herman pulled into the town's center in not one, not two, but three taxis in convoy. He rode in the first, his luggage traveled in the second, while his walking cane pulled up in the third. Everyone cheered at the sight of his grand entrance. Herman's high living continued unchecked, however, and grew increasingly flamboyant. Months later, after squandering every last penny, he was homeless. Like the vision of seeing the farm workers burn their money, Herman's sad story stayed with me.

When I was sixteen, Sylvia's younger brother, Shirley, moved in with us to help with the shop. At twenty-one, he was a lot older than I was, but I didn't mind. I welcomed the company, while Uncle welcomed the extra hands and eyes. He'd been growing increasingly frustrated by theft at the hands of a couple of his employees.

One Friday night, Shirley was getting ready to go to a party. It was the mid-fifties, and rock 'n' roll fever was in full swing throughout the island. House parties were all the rage. Did I, he asked, want to come along? The words were like magic in my ears. *A party?* I had never been to one of those. That night, I experienced rock 'n' roll from the corner in which I stood frozen the entire night. The following morning, Uncle Harrison marched right up to me. "Soh! You big man now!" Immediately I recognized my error and felt my tail go between my legs. My eyes hit the floor.

"No, Ahshook."

"Nes' time you feel ol' enough to leave withou' ask, you pack bag and go back to own faddah!"

"Yes, Ahshook."

That was the last time I ever stepped out of line with my uncle. A few weeks later he came to me again, this time with a question. It was one that would set me on my future's path. "Vincen'," he began, "Wha' you wan' do with studies? Wha' you wan' do aftah?" I was a little startled. He had never asked me anything about myself before. Not ever.

"I...I want to become a doctor, Ahshook," I replied, glancing only briefly at him, wondering if this was a joke of some kind. A few seconds passed before he replied. I could almost hear him assessing my answer.

"Thah' good profession," he said. "Buh' I make offah. If you stay here in shop, I give you own shop when you become a man. You think. You decide. You tell me ansah." With that, my uncle ended what was pretty much the longest conversation he and I would ever have.

That night I lay in my bed and stared at the ceiling. Outside, the crickets sang their evening song as a cool breeze drifted through the window. For as long as I could remember, I had seen myself as a doctor who healed cuts, mended bones, and got rid of pain. In fact, I had become close to a few other school friends with the same ambition. (Not only would they all go on to become doctors, my friend Dr. Ken Baugh would also hold office at one point as Jamaica's Minister of Health, and Deputy Prime Minister.) Becoming a doctor was what I had always wanted—or so I thought. Was it possible that Uncle saw something else in me?

There I was, still just a boy and being offered the chance to cut my path in a different direction. Confused, I wrote to my brother King. *Uncle has asked me to leave school and work for him instead. He has promised me a shop of my own when I become a man if I help him. What should I do?*

King was not happy. His reply arrived as quickly as the postman could deliver it. *No, Vin. Stay in school. I am earning money now, so I will pay your board and tuition from here on. When you become a doctor you can repay your uncle the rest.*

Not long after, King drove to Montego Bay to speak directly to Uncle Harrison. "Thank you, Uncle," he said. "You have been so kind to our family, but I will take care of Vincent now," he said. "None of us finished high school. He will be the first."

After King left, I continued to wrestle with the dilemma. I didn't know it, of course, but I had arrived at an unexpected crossroad. The truth was, deep down I was intrigued with the idea of working, and eventually having my own business. Having grown up in a shop, it felt natural to me. Becoming a doctor, while my lifelong dream, felt like an alien world.

King wanted to save me from shop life—its perpetual frustrations, backbreaking work, and punishing hours. That much I knew for sure. It was no small thing that he did, standing up to my uncle like that. Admittedly, my father's example was not the most encouraging. Having had the benefit of Uncle Harrison's example, however, I knew that the shop business didn't have to be a dead end. If my father had only chosen a better location, we could have done well too. Our family could have stayed together. Uncle Harrison's example showed me that, if done right, a business could succeed. But there was something else, too. I knew I was softhearted like my dad. If I did, in fact, become a doctor, I ran the risk of taking chickens and carrots for payment, just like he did.

For a while I struggled, but soon made my decision by looking at the wider picture: God had put Uncle Harrison in my path just when I needed the help. This uncle had given me food, shelter, and an education that went beyond books. Now it was my turn to help him by learning the way of life that had made his generosity possible. In what felt like outright defiance, I wrote King and told him my decision. I would leave school, and work with Uncle Harrison. I sent the letter, unhappy that I was disappointing my big brother, but convinced that I was making the right choice for me. I told my brother that everything would be all right. I told him so because I believed it.

Decades later—when we had become men—King would explain his reason for wanting me to stay in the classroom and step away from a life behind the counter. While he was still in high school and boarding with friends of the family, he had to go one night without dinner. The family simply did not call him to the dining table as they usually did. The next day he found out why: our father had failed to send them King's boarding fees that month. For that one lapse in payment, King went hungry for a night. He obviously survived—it was just one night—but he never forgot the feeling of going to bed with a growling stomach. He wanted to make sure the rest of us never had to miss a meal. Not if he could help it.

Like stepping into a new classroom, I began my official apprenticeship with Uncle Harrison. I never heard him say it, of course, but I could almost see him smiling deep (way down deep) inside. Now he'd allow his glances at me to linger a few seconds longer, or walk by a little closer as we worked together.

It was at about this time that I got confirmation that I was correct in my secret assessment of the ties between Aunt Sylvia and Uncle Harrison. I discovered this the day his wife arrived from China. A somewhat portly woman with shiny cheeks and a pleasant smile, her arrival had Uncle immediately on edge. No one had to tell me to stay out of everyone's way. That afternoon, I suddenly found an incredible amount of work in the yard that I just had to do.

Later that day, Uncle sent Sylvia to Kingston. For a couple weeks I struggled to hold happy thoughts in my mind. I had lost another mother. I promised myself that one day I would go to visit them both. That day would come sooner than I imagined. Some months later, after my seventeenth birthday, I received a letter from King. Our mother was well again and leaving the sanatorium. Our father's plan was to leave Claremont with

Winston and go to Kingston. He had managed to save some money, enough to try again at another shop, this time in the big city.

Almost a year later, King came to see me. His hesitation to greet me signaled that he came bearing bad news. I was right. Our father was struggling with his new shop. He was now asking me to come to Kingston to help. Just as Uncle did not show his pleasure when I chose to stay and work with him, he remained silent when I told him the news. Even though he was doing extremely well by this time, and even though we both knew I could not turn my back on my own father, Ahshook threw his glance away from me. With a sudden urgency, he began tending to something in the shop.

The day I left, my uncle and I parted with no words. To the man who had watched over me for seven years, I gave a slow and respectful nod. I managed a quiet "Good-bye, Uncle." I knew I'd miss him. For all his eccentric ways, he had shown me his own brand of kindness.

I didn't quite know how, but I knew I'd make it up to him someday.

CHAPTER 4

Toe in the water

"Train your eyes to see something where others see nothing. Look at Zhang Yin, the lady who became a billionaire in the 1990s by selling wastepaper scraps to cardboard manufacturers in China. She turned trash into treasure."

Vincent

I WAS ALMOST NINETEEN WHEN I ARRIVED IN Kingston for only the second time in my life. My parents' address in hand, I went straight to their small two-bedroom house atop their shop. I had not seen my father since the day he left for Claremont. Now sporting deep wrinkles, he looked tired, as did my mother. I was at once glad I came. The only children with them now were their oldest son, Que, George, who had left Anchovy to join them, and me. The other kids had either moved on in marriage, or had been formally adopted by their guardians, including little Winston. Mae came to see us once we settled in. She had also relocated to Kingston and was living on her own. King was still working with the bauxite company in the countryside, and doing well for himself.

Following the quiet reunion with my parents, I went to see Aunt Sylvia to let her know I had left Montego Bay. She looked restless, but smiled the entire time I was there, presenting me with treat after treat from her small kitchen, even though I kept declining politely. We did not speak about Uncle's wife, but spoke about Uncle, which seemed to make her eyes sparkle. I let her know of my plans to help my father in his new shop. She smiled and said she had no doubt that I would be a helpful son.

I was the new kid in town. With no time in which to get my bearings, I threw myself into the family's new enterprise and quietly assessed the situation. We were now operating in a city environment where competition was as robust as the island's famous coffee. I felt hope percolating in my veins. Maybe this was our chance to shine. We made it a full-fledged family effort—my parents and George worked during the day, and Que helped at nights. I covered both shifts.

Before long, I saw that, while we were bringing in some sales—considerably more than we had in Springfield—we were not exactly blazing a trail. Once I became familiar with the city,

I realized our error. Once again, it was location. We were not in the heart of the heaviest traffic, but along the outskirts in a relatively poor neighborhood.

My heart sank. I kept my angst to myself hoping that I was wrong. Perhaps we just needed more time. Telling ourselves that this was just a case of the usual growing pains, we worked day and night serving customers, while tweaking our range of goods to enhance sales. When Lynn Seung, a friend and fellow business owner, suggested we team up to boost our buying power, we began buying rice and oil at better prices. The strategy helped, but only marginally. My frustrations grew when I realized that Que's focus was not on growing our business, but on having fun. Sometimes, he wouldn't even show up for his shift. Admittedly, he had always been more of a lady chaser than anything else. That was cute when we were kids running around in Springfield shirtless and barefoot, but now we were young men with lives to forge. I tried to talk some sense into my brother, but we were simply too different. Ultimately, I knew I couldn't do anything to change or control him, so I focused on what I could control—me. I doubled my efforts behind the counter. All I wanted to see was even a hint of traction.

One day, like a sunbeam bursting through dark rain clouds, a most unexpected visitor appeared in our shop. I looked up from my spot behind the counter and saw a man standing in our doorway. It took me a few seconds to register the identity of the silent customer—it was Uncle Harrison. If

I had any doubts about the reason behind his visit, they vanished when he presented me with a gift—a popsicle maker like the one he used. At that point, I knew that all was well between us. I offered him a cool drink and showed him around our small place. The visit, which lasted less than five minutes, was an overdue booster shot. It reminded me that success, while maybe not within close reach, was still possible. I just had to stay the course.

Soon after, our landlord gave us notice. He had plans, he said, to repair his building and increase his rental income. I was both upset and relieved. I disliked the feeling of being kicked around like a football on our landlord's whim, even if it was his prerogative to do so. At the same time, however, I was happy for the excuse to find a better place.

Much to my dismay, our next location was even worse. We ended up in Rae Town, a notoriously rough area with a prison nearby. My father saw my quiet anxiety, but defended his choice by pointing to his shallow pockets. "Vin," a cousin tried to warn me, "Your old man is going in the wrong direction. He's not going to see any action there. He should be heading north. Any farther south and he'll end up in the harbor!"

In an attempt to turn things around, I decided to try something on my own while still working at my father's shop. With little money to my name for capital outlay, I had no choice but to start small. Following the example of a few, I decided to sell unused newspaper print, the same kind that grocery shops like ours used to wrap goods. Buying the paper for a song was easy; delivering it was not.

With help from a generous cousin who agreed to act as security for a small loan, I bought a new Morris van. Meanwhile, I negotiated a good price with the *Jamaica Gleaner* for the scrap paper. I began selling the day I got my van. I collected the paper, drove the load to my parents' shop, cut the sheets into squares right on our countertop, and started visiting prospective customers. I wasted nothing. I even took the bits and ends, cut them into tiny squares, and sold them to the *peaka-peow* guys, roadside purveyors of the then-popular unlicensed Chinese lottery-style gambling games.

My new venture was treading water at best. I was barely making my loan payments, much less a profit. While making deliveries, my eye was usually more focused on the gas gauge than the road itself, because I could only afford to fill the tank to the quarter mark. Tires were another luxury I could barely afford. I'd wear those out until the inner tubes burst.

One day, I finally got caught. While traveling down one of Kingston's busier arteries, the van began to sputter—I was out of gas. Luckily for me, Slipe Road sloped slightly downward. I quickly cut the engine and shifted the gear-stick van into neutral. My master plan was to piggyback on gravity and slip into the nearest gas station. Then my luck changed. At the bus stop, about two hundred feet ahead, stood my brother Que. There was my gas money in my future after all. I grinned and tapped the horn so that it gave a friendly honk. Que looked up from his newspaper and saw me. As I veered toward him he returned the smile, thrilled that he had just been saved a hot and crowded bus ride home. We both stopped smiling when he told me that, other than his bus fare, he had no money on him. I returned the next day with a gallon of gas, grateful that my van was still there with all four tires still attached.

The scrap paper business was not my future, that much I knew. It was only the first step in a much wider wading pool. I took it in stride and kept my eyes focused on the next opportunity. Meanwhile, I made the tough decision to cut ties with my father's shop. Brotherly love alone could not make the business relationship between Que and me work. It was going to hurt my father to hear the words, but I respected him enough to be truthful. Burying the issue under forced smiles and worn-out patience would only break us all in the long run. To his credit, not only did my father take it well, he let me go with his blessing. In that moment, I learned that the best gift you can give someone—and yourself—is the truth.

I was now twenty-two. My next step demanded more of my business muscle. Learning from my father's mistake, I set my sights north. I wanted something a little more uptown where customers had more disposable income. Eventually, I found a place with steady pedestrian traffic, and decided it would be perfect for a bread depot and ice-cream parlor. With a little help from King, I put aside enough for a couple months' rent. It stretched me financially, but I knew I had to go where customers had cash.

I finally had my own shop. Now I needed money for inventory—but all I had in my pockets was lint. Feeling as if I'd just been caught in an undertow, I began speaking to God a lot, asking for guidance. *Had I done the right thing? Did I move too quickly?* Meanwhile, with the rental agreement already in effect, the clock ticked.

There was only one thing to do: ask for help. I took a deep breath before approaching the same cousins who had previously stood as security for my loan. They owned a small bakery downtown, using the same dough-breaker my father had in Springfield. The difference was they had electricity, and a much better customer base. I sold them on my great location, and assured them that I'd be able to make my payments. They agreed to supply me with fresh bread daily as long as I paid them promptly at the end of each week. With my confidence bolstered, I approached another fellow who did pastries. Again I painted the picture of strong pedestrian traffic, which led him to make me the same offer. A third kind soul—a close friend— also came to my rescue.

Fred was an English fellow who owned a small carpentry shop. "Fred, I need a few simple shelves and fixtures," I said, "but I don't have much money. Would you help me out?" I showed him the sketches of what I wanted. He didn't hesitate.

He told me that if I got the lumber, he'd front me the carpenter's fees. I could pay him as soon as my cash flow picked up.

A month later, just before the next month's rent became due, I opened for business. I said several thank-you prayers to God for the family and friends who offered a hand when I needed it. To this day I can't remember giving my shop a name, only scrambling to give it life. Meanwhile, my father was pulling the plug on his shop. He'd finally given up. My heart ached for him. Even though I knew it was the practical thing to do, I wanted nothing more than for him to enjoy the taste of his own financial success, at least once in his life.

As the sole employee, I practically slept at my little shop, making the most of every waking minute to serve customers and make a profit. Soon, I could see the steady trickle turning into a small flow. I kept my word and had my creditors' money ready in sealed envelopes at the end of each week. I never made them wait. A quiet confidence replaced the slight apprehension I was nursing before. It was going to be all right, I told myself.

Then, early one morning, I got a visit from another cousin who owned a wholesale business. My father had been their customer. Now, he was their debtor. It was a matter of principle. As my name appeared on my father's business, my cousin said, his debt became mine. I couldn't—and didn't—argue. I repaid them monthly and erased our family's obligations. I learned then that bad debt—especially when past due—is about as palatable as rancid rice. It was not for me.

Somehow, though, I managed to build my own business while servicing my father's debt. A short side venture with a cousin also brought me some extra cash. Baron had come up with the idea of doing a Chinese-style jerk pork that we would sell as street food. At the time, the signature jerk treat was not as readily available as it is today. In those days, it was available to Kingstonians mainly on Friday evenings, thanks to a couple pioneering vendors who transported the tasty delicacy all the way in from the island's north coast. Baron said it was a tasty opportunity. I agreed.

We started small, putting together just enough money to buy twenty pounds of pork. A friend of ours with some culinary talent, who went by the name of Tarzan, took care of seasoning the meat. I took care of transporting the seasoned slab to my cousins who owned the downtown bakery. We timed it so that I'd arrive after their morning baking was over. Into their huge brick oven went our slathered pig—the same oven in which they baked their bread. I'm happy to say that standards in Jamaica for food preparation have evolved significantly since then. Those days were a bit like the wild West.

When our first round of roast pork sold like the last meal before a famine, we doubled our volume and kept going, selling every succulent morsel each time. I was so excited watching our venture grow, sleep began to feel like a waste of time. Then, our meat supplier ran into supply issues, causing us to lose precious momentum. I was disappointed but not deterred. The brief thrill of filling an untapped market was a rush I would not soon forget. Before long, word of our whirlwind rodeo got around, which had others approaching us with their own ideas. One came from a fellow who had just returned from New York. "Pizza, Vin! What about pizza? Do you think that could do well here? It's all over New York!"

"Could be an opportunity!" I said, eager to talk business. "But, ah…what the heck is pizza?"

America—there it was again. Even though my first business attempts had me springing out of bed each morning like a kid at Christmas, I still found myself wondering about life beyond the island's shores. The notion of America and the opportunities it held had remained glued to the back of my mind. The only hurdle was the right access to its gateway. I turned my thoughts to England. With the island's commonwealth ties still strong, all I needed was a passport. Soon, I gave in to curiosity, and wrote a friend in London asking if I could come and scout out the possibilities. He wrote back saying that he had just bought a two-bedroom flat. If I wanted it, the spare room was mine.

I let the idea of leaving flicker quietly in my mind. I told myself that it couldn't hurt to investigate new options across the pond. Meanwhile, opportunities at home were still sending out steady sparks. Cousin Baron had come back with yet another business proposal. This time, it involved a small but busy fast-food joint located across the university campus. The owner wanted to free his time so he could focus on a new venture he was exploring. All he wanted from us was the rent. The profit would be ours. "Just picture all those hungry students coming through our doors, Vinnie," Baron said, lightly pumping two clenched fists. "Man, we could really pull this off!"

I thought about it hard. There was no way I could carry two demanding businesses. This new venture meant taking an even bigger chance, especially for me. Up to that point, boiling an egg was as far as my cooking skills went, but I couldn't let that get in the way of the potential before us. Eventually, I went with my gut instincts and sold my first shop after only a year. The profit I came away with was small, but it was enough to cover my next step. I was happy with that, grateful that I had not lost my investment.

The restaurant, which we renamed *Doctor Bird*, took off nicely while nearly running us into the ground physically. We never stopped moving. If we weren't serving customers or working in the kitchen, we were racing behind the scenes to prepare for the next day's business. Restaurant work, I soon came to realize, was like being a stage performer—you were only as good as your last show. We stuck it out, though. After about a year of nonstop, backbreaking work, we built up sales strong enough to attract another buyer. We decided to take the offer while we were ahead. We'd had a good enough sprint. After we wrapped up, I decided that now was as good a time as any to leave for England. I applied for my passport and waited for the day when I could book my flight, and pack my bag.

One day soon after, I ran into an acquaintance. After the usual exchange of pleasantries, he mentioned that one of the island's dairy distributors was looking for commercial drivers. I can't remember why the conversation even went in that direction, especially as I was not looking for a job, but somehow it did. For that I will be forever grateful. "You should apply, Vinnie," he said. "They're always looking for good people."

Later that day I told a friend about the conversation. Joe, who was a little older than I was, said it sounded like a good opportunity. Something about his tone suggested that he was doing more than sharing a passing thought. "But, Joe," I said, "I'm waiting for my passport to go to England." That's when I received a piece of advice that would forever change my life. It would be one of several.

"Vin, while you're busy waiting for your passport, go and make some money. You know how it is with time—once it's gone, you can't ever get it back."

Joe was right, of course. His advice reminded me that if I saw room on the stove for another pot, I should throw one on and get cooking. The next day I went in for the interview, and left with a job. I was now a milkman.

My debut as an employee started off on a shaky note. I joined the company in the middle of a strike, and then joined the handful of workers who had decided to cross the picket line. I knew it would make me the unpopular new guy, but I didn't worry about that. Someone had given me the opportunity to earn a living and I was not about to waste it. Twice a day I had to inch through the human barrier that blocked the entrance. The weekly pay—£6—made the harassment and potential physical harm worth it. That was relatively decent money back then.

I made my deliveries without fail. After a few months, I noticed a change in my paycheck—£8. I went to my boss Victor and pointed out the mistake. He was the brother who took care of the administrative side of the business.

"No," Victor said with a small grin. "It's not an error. It's your reward for being a good worker."

I was twenty-four and finally making a little money. I drove that delivery van five days a week, fueled by the promise of making a nice commission for doing a good job. I watched as my meager scrapings morphed into actual savings. When my passport finally arrived, I slipped it into my side drawer. I didn't quite have a plan, but I knew I needed to be here for the time being.

I had no clue just how right I was. Unbeknownst to me, a couple years before I joined the local dairy company, a much larger American counterpart had bought shares in it. Hailing from another island—Long Island City, New York—the overseas dairy giant was none other than Beatrice Foods Company. The business deal that transpired in the boardroom would become my steppingstone to America. When I learned of the affiliation, I immediately went to my other boss, Alex. I was a little closer to him, and shared with him my hopes of working in America. I asked if he thought I could apply to Beatrice Foods for a job. Maybe they'd even sponsor me, I suggested.

Once again I was the recipient of another's generosity. "Vinnie, it's a great idea," he said with a smile and a heavy sigh. "I'd hate to lose you, of course, but a hard worker like you would do well in the States. No question." He paused, seeming to consider his next sentence. "Jamaica is going to change soon, I'm afraid. It might take a while for things to settle down. If you're serious about the States, sure, I'll help set up the interview with Beatrice. I have some friends in the Bronx you can stay with. They'll meet you at the airport. Go and see if you like it. If things don't work out, you'll always have your job here."

To this day I thank God for Alex. He said the words that absolved me of any guilt I harbored about leaving my family and beloved homeland. Thanks to his encouragement, I took that crucial step toward my future. The day I applied for my visa at the US embassy, Alex took the tie from around his neck and handed it to me. When he realized from my shy confusion that I had never used one before, he gave a little smile, retrieved the tie from my hands, and put it around my collar. "Image matters, Vinnie, especially where you're going," he said as his hands worked the tie into a perfect Windsor knot. "Always remember that. Good luck at the embassy."

I got my visa with little effort. The timing could not have been better. For some years leading to this point, storm clouds had been gathering over the island's political landscape. With its umbilical cord from mother England cut in 1962, the infant nation was still taking its first few shaky steps. Then in 1965, the year after I'd joined the company, simmering anti-Chinese sentiment resurfaced. Riots broke out through the streets of Kingston like a rash. Angry demonstrators looted and burned Chinese-owned businesses. It was the third eruption of its kind in fifty years. This time, however, many in the Chinese community decided to cast their sights on other countries—particularly the United States and Canada. I was among them. I made a silent promise that, while I would leave the island's shores, I would never turn my back on it. I would remain a faithful son.

And, so, with the help of someone whose generosity of spirit opened that first real door of opportunity, I got my visa and bought my airplane ticket. The barefoot kid from Springfield was going to America's largest city.

The year was 1967. I was twenty-seven.

PART TWO

The apple that caught my eye

CHAPTER 5

Preparing for the test

"I tell people all the time—if you really want to know the value of a penny, go to the bank with ninety-nine cents and see if they'll give you a dollar in exchange. They won't."

Vincent

I WAS SO EXCITED ABOUT MY FIRST PLANE RIDE that I gave little thought to the fact that I was soaring miles above the earth. When the flight attendants came around with their carts offering drinks, I asked for a beer, not realizing that I had to pay for it. In fact, I had no American dollars on me.

I began to hand it back in apology, when the passenger next to me insisted on buying me the beer. He was a slightly older gentleman, traveling with his family. "First time?" he asked as he gave the money to the flight attendant. I nodded with an embarrassed smile as I thanked him for his help. He gave a kind look as he unfolded his newspaper. "Don't mention it. So…New York, huh?"

"Yes, sir," I said.

"Brace yourself, young chap. A great city it is, but a tough world to live in for sure. There's no other place on Earth quite like it."

I listened quietly, taking note of the deep respect my fellow passenger had for our destination. It was genuine encouragement tempered with a subtle warning. He continued talking, this time turning to look me in the eye.

"If you haven't already heard it, there's a famous saying about New York: if you can make it here, you can make it anywhere." I washed down his words with my beer. From the way it was sounding, the real ride was going to take place once I landed.

From the moment I set my feet on American soil that pleasant November day, I was hooked. Everything I saw, heard, and felt was unlike anything I'd ever experienced. *Everything* made an impression on me. JFK International Airport looked like an anthill that had just been disturbed. People in the hundreds were scurrying in every which way, speaking in languages that were new to my ears. Never had I seen that many bodies in one place.

My New York contacts met me at the airport as planned. On the drive in, I almost got whiplash trying to inhale it all: bold bridges that stretched across bodies of water like rubber bands; trains that raced side by side before breaking away into opposite directions; statuesque buildings that seemed to catapult themselves to the sky; and wide roadways that rose from the ground and crisscrossed overhead. The streets were alive with shiny vehicles, and pedestrians of several races, all united in the same hurried pace, all moving with purpose in their stride. Along our route I saw businesses of different kinds. Some were large, with lofty signs and entranceways that waved and beckoned. Others were small and simple, often shoehorned between bigger buildings. All vied for the public's attention.

Try us!

Stop here!

We're the best!

Meanwhile, my host, who was doing a great job at pointing out the city's iconic landmarks, apologized for the frustrating traffic. I didn't see inconvenience, though. I saw action. I sensed opportunity. I heard the cash register ringing every few minutes. By the time we arrived at his house, my mind wouldn't stop racing. *This is it*, I told myself. *This is where I need to be.*

The Beatrice Foods interview, while encouraging, did not lead to a job. I returned to Jamaica feeling anything but disappointed. I had seen enough to know that my childhood instincts about America had been right. I applied for another visa as quickly as I could. While waiting, I relocated my parents back to the countryside so that King could take care of them. They were getting on in age and had little energy now for a family-run business. I told my brother that even though New York looked like it could swallow me whole, I desperately wanted to take a crack at it. As badly as I wanted to go, my brother's opinion was still important to me. This time, I wanted his blessing. This time, he was ready to give it. "Vin, you're doing the right thing," he said. "You're young. Go see what's out there. I'll help you however I can." He ended with the same words I told him when I dropped out of school. "It'll be all right." I packed all the clothes I owned. Just like before, everything fit perfectly in one small suitcase.

The company you seek reflects your inner image. That's why it's important to surround yourself with family, friends, and associates you admire—quality individuals with whom you share similar goals, standards, and attitudes. Not only will they bring out the best in you, they will support your belief that a brilliant sun sits above even the darkest clouds.

When I returned to New York the following February, the winter I'd been hearing about had already arrived. This time my friends met me with a loaner coat. What greeted me outside barely resembled the world I had seen only a few months before. Now the sky was gray and low. The trees, once beautiful with magnificent leaves, were now bare and brown. I stared through the car window wondering what mysterious disease had eaten away at them. I also noticed that the cars seemed to have developed muffler problems—there was certainly a good deal of smoke coming from the tailpipes. In fact, there was a good deal of "smoke" coming from pedestrians' mouths too!

About a week after my arrival, I landed a job. My good fortune came through my hosts, who decided to have a little house party. That Saturday night I met one of their guests. Jack was a fellow Jamaican who worked in the shipping department of a briefcase factory. He told me he knew of an opening at his workplace on the production line. If I was interested, he said, he would introduce me to his boss that Monday. I wrote the directions to the intersection where we'd meet.

At eight that Monday morning I was shaking hands with Jack's boss. Joe was a tall, slim, Jewish American with a heavy New York accent. He and his brother, Bernie, ran their family's second-generation business, located on Bathgate Avenue in the Bronx. "I understand you're looking for a job," Joe said, sizing me up. "So you speak English then?"

I smiled. It didn't occur to me then, but Joe was likely having difficulty reconciling my Asian face with my country of birth. "Yes, it's the only language I know."

He gave a small nod. "I assume you don't mind hard work?"

"Been working since I was a boy, sir."

"And you're OK with factory work."

"If it produces, I'm fine with it."

I guess I answered with enough conviction, because he hired me immediately. "Welcome to Carry Case," he said with the tone of an individual with a long day ahead of him. "Take your jacket off and go see Frank, our foreman. He'll get you settled in."

That was the extent of my job interview. I was so shy I didn't even ask what the job paid. I didn't care, quite frankly, it was a job. With that, my new life began.

I still remember the excitement of making my debut in the United States and its iconic city. I felt as if I'd just been allowed into the most sought-after club. I knew that, if given the chance, I would do right by this great nation. I was here for the giving, not the taking. That was not in my DNA. About the only thing I meant to take was the opportunity to make something of myself so that I could return the favor. I was going to live my life in such a way that others would point at me, and say, "Now there goes a fine American."

I was now employed. Regardless of how bad the weather was, or how I was feeling, I clocked in every morning at 7:00 a.m. sharp to begin a full day's work. I still remember the numbers that shaped my life during this period. I was earning minimum wage then, $1.60 an hour. My weekly pay was sixty dollars. Tax was eleven. As soon as I brought home my forty-nine dollars, I'd put aside money for a week's worth of train tokens so I could return to work. Tokens were twenty cents each. Next came my rent, electricity, and telephone—thirty dollars. I survived on whatever was left.

I sacrificed any way I could. I ate simply, rarely seeing the inside of a restaurant. When I learned that you could get fish heads for free at the local fish market, I became a regular customer. (The vendors have long since caught on.) For my train commute I took the longer route, which involved taking three trains. The first train, the 5, took me downtown to 180th Street. From there I'd catch the 2 train going uptown to White Plains Road and Gunhill Road. From that stop, I'd catch the Third Avenue train. That was my daily commute: three long trains on one cheap fare. It was more economical than taking the shorter line, which would have chopped my travel time by half. The daily savings, albeit marginal, translated significantly when multiplied by five. That's the beauty about numbers: they tell a story in a way that words sometimes cannot.

I didn't stop there. I ignored the temptation of the shopping culture and bought only what was necessary to cover and keep me warm. I owned one winter jacket, a pair of gloves, and one hat. There were no movie nights and no pub stops. (I did, however, eventually splurge on my first slice of pizza.)

I even picked up coins off the ground when I came across them. They were mostly pennies, of course, but I reached for them anyway. To me it was honest money for which I held noble intentions. Each time I saw one waiting for me, I felt a quiet appreciation for the small gift. None of the sacrifices bothered me. I knew the pain would be temporary. The truth was, I enjoyed saving. Each time I found a way to keep my money instead of giving it to someone else, I felt smarter for it.

I'm still addicted to saving and wise spending. Wasteful spending to me is like meat to a vegetarian—it makes me queasy. It's not that I deprive myself. Nowadays, if I want something, not only will I get it if I can comfortably afford it, I will buy top quality. When I do so, however, it's for me, not for the Joneses. That's just not my style.

Even today, with each dollar I spend I think about what it took for me to earn it. Which is why it pains me to see hard-working paycheck-to-paycheck people fork out a week's pay for a pair of shoes, tickets to a sporting event, or the latest gadget. It's a mindset that chafes me to the core. I encourage young people all the time to exercise self-discipline with the money they worked so hard to earn.

If you don't have your priorities straight, sort them out fast. Don't drive a luxury car or wear designer clothes and shoes when you have no place to sleep, or no padding in your savings account. Avoid a deficit like your life depends on it, because it does. I share this message with anyone who will listen. It is the one rule of thumb I've seen many fail to grasp, no matter how many times it comes close to strangling them. Humble yourself, I say. Humble yourself. When the dealership writes to suggest that I change out my eight-year-old Mercedes for the newest model, I'll politely decline. I'll keep that car for another couple years as long as it's in good shape.

After a few months on the job, Mr. Joe came up to me one day while I was on my break. The name *Mr. Joe* was a compromise on my part. Everyone called him Joe. As a new transplant, however, I was still more comfortable with the formal West Indian way of greeting strangers and superiors: Mr., Mrs., or Ms. and the last name. In time, though, I came to appreciate, and prefer, the more relaxed American way of interacting with people. It taught me that it is possible to call someone by his or her first name and still show respect. Today, I'm very American that way.

"Vinnie," said Mr. Joe, "I like the way you work. You're painfully punctual and always giving us more than a hundred percent. You work as if you own the place."

"Thank you, sir," I said, grateful for the recognition. Thinking that the conversation was over, I got up to return to the assembly line, but stopped when he spoke again.

"So I'm giving you a raise. No one else is getting one." Then he told me I'd be getting an extra dime an hour. Encouraged by the reward, I seized the opportunity to ask if there was overtime work available. I had not asked before because no one seemed to do any. What I didn't realize, however, was that no one wanted it. Mr. Joe, also a nonstop worker, smiled in approval. "Well, all right then, Vin, tell you what. When everyone's gone at the end of the day, go down to the warehouse, start straightening up, and I'll come tell you what we need done."

I continued working at Carry Case, grateful for my start. That summer, I started looking for a better paying job in earnest. When I told Mr. Joe of my plans to move on, he offered to double my pay. It was incredibly generous of him, and I felt uncomfortable for declining, but I knew I could do better. I had just turned twenty-nine—I *had* to do better. So, I turned to my sidewalk pennies. At the time, *The New York Post* cost eight cents. I bought a copy and combed the job ads.

Before long, I found a Bronx-based company by the name of Chesterfield Farms. Located on East 233rd Street, they were looking for deliverymen. I smiled at the irony of working for yet another dairy company. I decided that it had to be a sign, and called for the details. The hours were grueling—2:00 a.m. to 8:00 a.m.—but the pay started at $148 weekly. I applied and was hired on the spot. *Not a bad return for sidewalk pennies*, I thought. Before leaving Carry Case, I thanked Mr. Joe for the chance to get on my feet. We shook hands as we wished each other well. I could not have known then that there would be another factory in my future.

My new job with the dairy company had a few immediate challenges. The first had to do with a minor cultural difference. "Vinnie, go to the garage and bring down truck number thirty-four," said my new supervisor on my second day.

When I got to the bay, however, all I saw were panel vans. I reported my findings to my boss—there were no trucks in the garage, only vans. That's when I learned that, in America, anything that wasn't a car was pretty much a truck. Once in my "truck," I had to learn my way around the city, and fast. I caught on quickly enough, but not before stopping many a policeman to ask for directions. Fortunately, most were accommodating.

The other challenge was physical. Most of my deliveries were to walk-up dwellings. I spent most of my nights climbing stairs—four, sometimes five flights per stop. At first I thought nothing of it. I was young and energetic, quite unlike the clunker I was assigned to drive, which was old and tired and covered with scrapes and dents like age spots. The ultimate challenge came, however, when winter arrived. Since the delivery stops were only seconds apart, the truck's folding door was never closed for long, if at all, so I never had a chance to get warm.

That first winter, I secretly wondered if I would survive New York. The hairs in my nostrils felt like stalactites. I was sure the cold would slice clean through my bones, and that, one night, I'd be found comatose with my hands frozen to the steering wheel. I did, in fact, almost lose my big toes one night after a fresh snowfall. At the time I was wearing regular leather shoes, as I hadn't yet bought winter boots. Each time I trudged through the light snow, some flew into my shoes like wet dust. When I walked into my apartment the following morning, my toes were blue. The next day, the nails fell off.

That weekend I wrote to a cousin in San Diego about possibly moving there. She was moving to Canada, she replied, but said that I was welcome to use her house. It was tempting. I thought about it hard, but decided to stick it out. I told myself that I needed to go with my first impression—the one that told me that New York was the place to be. *Just stay on track*, I told myself. *You'll get your reward in due time.*

I continued working like a possessed man, even putting in some extra time at the gas station on the premises. I'd stay back to refill the gas tanks, and grease the trucks' wheel-well springs, a task that had me working under the trucks for about two or three hours after my deliveries. It meant sleeping a little less, but earning a little more.

Night after long night I reported for work. I disciplined myself into a no-excuses mindset, no matter how bad it got out there—and sometimes it got pretty awful. One night, a snowstorm slammed the area without warning, causing even some trains to stop running, but my customers still woke up the next morning to find their milk at their doorstep. On another night, sleet blanketed the borough while I was in the middle of my route. Minutes later I hit a patch of black ice. I gripped the steering wheel as my truck skated into a snow bank like steel to a magnet. I had no choice but to lock the truck and walk home. That was the only night I didn't deliver. As my customers had enjoyed reliable service up to this point, however, they were quick to forgive me. Most showed their appreciation through their generous Christmas tips. In all my years as a New York milkman, I know of only two customers I disappointed.

The first was an elderly lady in her sixties who lived in an apartment building. As was my routine, I collected payment from my customers every other Saturday. This lady was always ready with a few minutes' conversation, which I didn't mind, as long as I had the time to spare.

One Saturday she invited me in for a meal. She had made chicken, she said, and since I had to eat at some point, I should sit with her for a short break. I thought it would be rude to decline, particularly as she had been a pleasant customer, so I politely accepted, emphasizing that I couldn't stay long. The meal, while hot, was the blandest thing I'd ever tasted. Still, I was grateful for her thoughtfulness. When I got up from the table and tried to leave, however, she ran to the door and blocked it, her face and body language revealing her real motive behind the "kind offer." That's when I realized what the free meal was really all about. I made it past her somehow and never returned.

The second incident was with a doorstep customer in Mount Vernon. After a few months of delivering without incident, I began to notice the fellow peeping through his window each morning just as I pulled up. I found it odd, but figured he didn't want anyone stealing his milk. After all, New York could be a little rough in those days. Then, one morning, just as I was placing the bottle on the floor, he opened the door with a hopeful smile on his face and appendage to match in his pants. I didn't return there either.

Then there were the work hazards. On two occasions, for instance, I was held up at gunpoint while delivering in the projects. I was alone the first time. Knowing better than to hit the streets with cash on my person, however, I had no money to give. Instead, I showed the would-be robber the change in my pockets. He assaulted me with the basic menu of curse words as I drove off. A block later, I saw a cop and sent him after the guy.

A cousin from out of town was riding with me, and witnessed the second attempt. This time the robber was older. When he produced his gun, I feigned an apology. "Man, I'm sorry. I don't carry a wallet, just my driver's license. I have a check in my pocket, though. You want that?" The robber scowled.

"So you're a smart aleck, huh?" Then he waved the gun at my poor cousin, who tossed his wallet out the window before yelling at me to hit the gas.

I was happy in my new home. To me, New York was a giant classroom. Each day was different. Each scenario taught you something new. It was the larger message, however, that had transformed me into an eager student on the edge of his seat—I saw that here, you had the freedom to chart your own course. I saw that a man could live a pretty good life in America, even as a blue-collar worker. I came to that conclusion after meeting a fellow who was a sanitation worker in the city. This man had been able to save enough money, not just to live a comfortable life, but to buy a home *and* an investment property. He did all that on a garbage collector's pay. While I didn't know much about the world then, I knew that that couldn't happen as easily in too many other countries, including the one I was born in. There, the circumstances of your birth usually determined the circumstances of your life.

I saw that, in America, it was possible to start life at one end of the spectrum and still reach for the other. In America, you could be born to parents with no wealth, no power, and no privilege, and yet grow up to possess all three. You could get there if you tried hard enough and kept your head on straight. You could do that because, in America, the only thing to stop you from succeeding was you.

All you needed to do was ask yourself two questions: *What do you want? And how badly do you want it?*

CHAPTER 6

Gathering friends, building courage

"If there's one bit of advice I'd offer young people, it would be to start your adventure early. Take your chances in your youth if you can—your energy *will* wane with age even if your enthusiasm and intellect remain robust. This may sound ridiculous to an invincible twenty-five-year-old able to power through the day on four hours' sleep, but wise is the young man or woman who heeds this warning."

Vincent

I HAD NOW BEEN IN THE UNITED STATES FOR A FEW years. After working as an assembly line worker in a briefcase factory, I was now a milkman. I kept my family and friends back home current with my progress, mostly by airmail, of course. Still practicing self-discipline by saving every penny possible, I limited long distance calls to emergencies and special occasions. By living lean, I was able to buy a secondhand car for only $375. I had seen the "For Sale" sign stuck on the window one day as I headed home from work—it was, as fate would have it, a 1964 Dodge Polara.

The one person I did not stay in touch with was Uncle Harrison. It wasn't that I didn't think of him; he was never far from my mind. I simply knew that he would not be receptive to that kind of gesture. I did regularly correspond with Lynn Seung, however, the friend with whom my father and I had teamed up to buy goods in bulk when we were both shop owners in Kingston. Naturally, I asked Lynn how his business was faring, and how life was going for him in general. One day he replied with bad news. With the island's politics heating up, business was melting away. Unless the situation improved, he said, he would soon have to declare bankruptcy. The good news was that his wife had already migrated to the States and filed papers for him. "Come up when you can," I wrote back. "I can help get you a job with my company if you want. It's not an easy life, but there's more opportunity here in a city block than anywhere else in the world. Plenty for all if you're willing to work hard." And, so, my friend came to New York.

One day, sometime after, a coworker happened to mention seeing a small property for sale in the nicer part of the Bronx—a modest two-story building with two stores and four apartments. I investigated the prospect, and discovered that the asking price was reasonable. In those days, New York real estate was not the prohibitive feat that it is today. I checked my position—I had $5,000 in savings. *Not bad for a milkman's pay,* I thought, *but not enough for a deposit.*

I wrote King and asked if he'd consider buying the property with me. Once again my brother shored up my instincts. If I thought it was a good idea, he wrote, he was in. We jumped at it. A few weeks later I was a first-time property owner. I couldn't stop smiling. My brother and I had done something our father never could. However, I didn't break open a can of soda over it, much less the proverbial bottle of champagne. The rent barely covered the mortgage and expenses. In the end, given the hours I spent as landlord, plumber, and general repairman, it was hardly worth the financial risk. Sometimes, though, you have to pay for experience. We soon sold the property, and walked away with a small profit.

My brother is my unsung hero. I will be forever grateful to him for putting the wind in my sail during those early years. Were it not for his own self-discipline of sacrifice, hard work, and long-term thinking, he would not have been in a position to help me.

Soon after King and I sold our investment, I made a similar one with my friend Lynn. He, too, had managed to accumulate some savings, and wanted to give real estate investment in New York a try. I agreed to the joint venture, thinking that having a local partner would make it easier. We bought something—also small—but this time in a more downscale part of town, where the price was much lower. The purchase turned out to be a mistake. Collecting rent was erratic at best. The repairs and other duties, while now shared with my partner, still ate away most of my spare time. I chalked it up to another lesson learned.

By now I had been at the milk route for almost three years, working in the dark, battling the weather, and climbing those stairs. I was exhausted. One morning, I woke up to the rude shrill of the telephone. With my eyes still shut, I threw my hand over the table to reach for it. "Hello?" I said, sounding as if I'd been up all night drinking. No answer. I opened my eyes. In my hand was the alarm clock.

The final straw came closer to the end of my fourth year. New York was still in winter's grip. I had just made my last stop for the night—a doorstep delivery at a house with a small porch. After placing the bottle by the door, I turned to head back down the short flight of steps to the truck. But my legs, now like cement columns, would not move. It was so cold, it almost hurt to breathe.

I leaned against the wall, slid to the icy ground, and sat there. The wind cut a frigid swath across the porch. I shivered, pulled my scarf over my mouth, and closed my eyes. *Enough,* I said to myself. *There has to be a better way to make a living. I won't last much longer like this.* Then my mind drifted to the passenger on the plane, and the words he said to me that day. *If you can make it here, you can make it anywhere.* I took two deep breaths, willed my legs to work again, and headed back to the truck.

In the weeks that followed, I took another look at the landscape of options. Eventually, my mind turned to my shop-keeper roots. One morning, on my way home from work, I stopped by a nearby superette. I had become friendly with the owner, and thought I could get some advice from him. "Roger," I said, the circles visible under my eyes. "If you don't mind my asking, how does one go about getting a place like this?" His reply was immediately discouraging. Between the rent, light, insurance, and taxes, he said it was not something he'd recommend to anyone.

At first his answer surprised me. He'd been there for as long as I'd been working my route. If it was really that bad, why was he still at it? Then it occurred to me that perhaps he just didn't want to hand over his hard-earned information.

I decided not to take it personally. Not only was his protective measure his prerogative, I understood—and respected—the reason behind his hesitation. It was not easy out there. After years of jostling for a place at the table, getting elbowed by the competition overnight was a real possibility if you weren't careful. Why feed the hand that could bite you? *Law of the jungle,* I told myself. *Fair enough.* So I thanked him, wished him well, and left. Years later, a close friend of his would seek me out for advice about his own new business. Perhaps it was naive of me, but I told him just about everything I knew.

Meanwhile, the bottled milk business was succumbing to changing times. Its supermarket box-carton cousin was now much cheaper, and, therefore more appealing.

The demand for delivered bottled milk soured. In an attempt to halt the slide in sales, we switched from bottles to cartons, but those customers still clinging to tradition did not like the compromise. They liked neither the taste of delivered carton milk nor its price. If they were forced to buy carton milk, they said, then it had better be for less. Otherwise, they'd stop buying it altogether. My customers realized this was not good news for me. Most apologized with worried frowns. I told them I understood their position, and that I'd do the same. They were preaching to the choir, after all. With the writing on the wall, I decided to apply for a job with Dannon.

One morning soon after, I happened to arrive at work earlier than usual. Waiting inside was the company's owner. I raised my eyebrows in surprise. In my four years there, I had only seen him a handful of times. "Come here a minute, son," he said, beckoning with his hand. "I hear you're thinking of leaving us."

"Yes, sir," I said going slightly red in the face.

"I'm really sorry to hear that. You're one of our better workers. May I ask why the decision?" I explained that with sales dwindling as they were, I had little choice. I needed an income that moved up, not down. He nodded in agreement. "Fair enough," he said. "Can't say I blame you. Which is why I have a proposition I hope you'll consider." His plan seemed simple and fair to both sides: he would give me the same old clunker of a truck I'd been using, and pay me $200 for a six-day week, without benefits. I would buy the milk, eggs, and butter from the company and sell them for whatever price I wished. The profit was mine. If at the end of the year I could show that I had not made a minimum profit of $10,000, the company would reimburse me the difference.

I had not anticipated the offer. As life's impeccable timing would have it, Dannon returned to me that same week with a job offer: $150 for a five-day week, plus benefits.

For days I sat and stared at the two routes before me: one read *safe and basically straight.* The other, *risky winding roads but potentially rewarding.*

Dannon's offer was tempting. Dannon was a strong company with a popular product and an equally bright future. I knew I could do well there as long as I put in the time and effort. Eventually, I'd make that climb up the ladder. I was, after all, prepared to give them my usual 110 percent.

For a while I toyed with the picture of going home each night and sleeping soundly, knowing that I had the comfort of a steady paycheck and benefits, plus a nice pension for my old age. I had to admit that the vision of that safety net felt like an electric blanket on a frigid night. Yet, still, I couldn't stop wondering, *Vincent, what if you gave yourself that 110 percent?*

Days later I went back to my boss and accepted his offer. It turned out to be a bad move in the short term, of course, but I was not surprised. Home-delivered dairy was seeing the end of an era. To make things worse, the weather got so cold a couple times the following winter, the bottles cracked. I replaced them, of course, which I had to do at my own expense. Then there was the issue of the quart of oil the old truck needed every day to keep going. It was like a hospital patient on a drip.

Yet, with all that, I neither panicked nor regretted turning down a safe future with Dannon. Everything in my bones told me I was making the right choice. I knew in my heart that I wanted to call my own shots. I wanted to be an entrepreneur. All I needed to do from here on was to commit to that vision, and expect it to happen. The decision to stay the course still ranks to this day as one of the most pivotal of my life.

Sometimes it's hard following those whispered messages from God. It can be especially confusing when the other choice on the table seems safer or, worse, more logical. Those can be some of the toughest moments. You grapple with yourself. Do you go this way? Or do you go that way? All you can really do is to look within, and listen, really listen, to what your gut is telling you.

Not long after, a friend who was working at a Queens-based milk company approached me about a job. Dairy Lea needed what was called a "checker." Instead of hitting the road each night, I'd be checking inventory on the trucks before they rolled out to retail supermarket customers. I decided to accept it so I could take a little time to thaw out and breathe. At that point I was sure of two things: one, my stay at this company would be short-lived. Two, I was meant to be a business owner. I needed to think through my next move. I was all right with not having the whole plan mapped out in front of me; that would reveal itself in time. All I needed to be sure of was that next step.

It was during this time that I took care of two issues that had been gnawing at me. The first was my education. I had some unfinished business in the classroom, so I signed up to take classes for my GED. For peace of mind, I needed to complete that chapter in my life. I squeezed in the time before heading to work. It was while in the classroom that I discovered my astigmatism, and the reason I so frequently squinted to see. I didn't have the extra money, though, so glasses would have to wait until much later.

My other itch was family. I longed to see mine. I missed seeing their faces and hearing their voices for more than a couple minutes at a time. Incredibly, five busy years had passed since I left home. I booked my ticket, threw a few simple gifts in my suitcase, and hopped on a flight. When I landed in Montego Bay weeks later, I couldn't stop staring at the emerald sea. As for the beach, I had forgotten how white the sand looked under the shining sun. It looked like warm snow.

On my way in from the airport, I stopped by Uncle Harrison's shop for a visit. By now he had married Sylvia, and bought the building from his former landlord. As I intended to stay only briefly, I summed up my new life in a few efficient sentences. This was Uncle Harrison, after all. In the years since we last saw each other, he had not changed much. He responded in his usual manner, with a few nods and low grunts. This time, however, I caught him stealing several glances at me. I can only assume that it was because *I* had changed. No longer was I the young apprentice son.

I devoted the rest of my short vacation to my parents, my sister Nuke, and her husband, Ken. King was working in another parish and was, therefore, unable to join us, but we spoke at length on the phone. As for Winston, the youngest, he had by then left Jamaica to make a life in Trinidad and Tobago. My father still looked strong even though he had clearly aged. Then there was my mother. She was now blind, a result of her diabetes, but that didn't stop her from smiling at the sound of my voice when I walked into their house. She made me sit next to her for the next few days, her hand often squeezing mine, her face beaming with pride. I ate with my family, drank tea, and entertained them with stories of my American adventure, describing what it was like to live and work as a New Yorker. More importantly, I let them know that I was happy. As I said my good-byes on my last day, my mom surprised me with the longest hug she'd ever given me. I remember marveling at how strong she felt. It was as if she'd saved all her energy for that one embrace. I'm glad I visited when I did. Only a few months later, after a lifetime of struggling with her disease, my beloved mother passed away.

I eased into my new job at Dairy Lea like butter on warm toast. Acclimating to life in America had been almost as easy, save for a few train and subway incidents that made me question my ability to master this metropolis. That included the time a cousin of mine and I used an elevated train as an early "GPS." We were in Queens that day, and had to find our way to the Bronx. Instead of taking the Bronx-bound train, however, we decided to just follow it in our car. Our brilliant plan was working well, until the darned thing disappeared into a tunnel.

Assimilating as a visible minority had also been relatively event-free. It wasn't because I had practice at being a minority in my own country, nor was it due to the fact that I could blend into New York's large Chinese-American population. (And if you don't believe me, just imagine ordering dim sum as a man who looks as Chinese as Mao but speaks English with the accent of Bob Marley.) No, I believe I got along just fine because I chose to look past any obstacles that came my way, including racism.

My first encounter with racism in America had been indirect. It happened soon after I first arrived, when I had gone to see about an apartment for rent. The building's white superintendent showed me around on my first visit. He was pleasant enough, and even made an effort to chat a bit. After asking me a couple questions, he said that the place was mine if I wanted it. Still being new in town, I thought it would be good to get a second opinion, and so returned the next day with a friend who happened to be black. Much to my surprise, the apartment, to which I practically had the keys the day before, was suddenly "unavailable." If that felt like a slap in the face to me, then I can only imagine what that felt like to my friend.

If I was confronted with racism in America—and I have no doubt I was—I paid it little attention. I am not suggesting that racism is acceptable. It isn't. On this particular issue, however, my rule of thumb is to take each person as an individual, and not part of a large group. We all have our own learning curve where prejudice (of any kind) is concerned. I choose to live my truth quietly. It's my way of showing others who I am. Some may find this approach too laid-back. I admit that stronger action is sometimes needed. My preferred approach has more to do with my personality, however. I always gravitate first to tranquility.

I was now thirty-four, and anxious to take my life to another level. It was time to settle down with a family of my own. I just needed to find the right partner.

One night, I went to a friend's party. It had been a while since I'd done anything that didn't involve some form of work, so I was grateful for the light distraction. By the time I arrived, most of the guests were already there. It looked like it was going to be a nice blended gathering of American and Caribbean folks. Music competed with loud chatter as guests mingled and flocked to the snack table and makeshift bar. I shook hands with new faces, happy to add more friends and acquaintances to my list. Networking, I had discovered, was the trick to keeping homesickness at bay in such a vast city.

That evening, smiles abounded, tasty potluck meals filled bellies, and drinks flowed. I was immediately glad that I had accepted the invitation. Grabbing a paper plate, I indulged in the tasty offerings on the table while chatting with friends.

I had secured my first job in America thanks to a similar gathering. Little did I know that this party would open another door. This time, though, I didn't come away with the number of a prospective employer. This time, I left with the number of a pretty, petite nursing student with long dark hair, who was having a good time on the dance floor with her friends. Her name was Jeanie.

CHAPTER 7

Embracing life's flow

"Surround yourself with like-minded people, especially when it comes to choosing a life partner and close friends. Life is an unchartered ocean. It will get choppy at times. Having the support of those who believe in you and think as you do will help with navigating those rough waters."

Vincent

TIMING, THEY SAY, IS EVERYTHING. WHEN JEANIE and I met, we were both ready to settle down. She was studying to become a nurse, while I was working to build a base. Like me, she hailed from a large Chinese-Jamaican family and had grown up the child of shop owners. Like me, she had also lost her mother to diabetes. The comfort of our common backgrounds put me at ease.

Jeanie's family and friends felt differently, however. While Jeanie had a college education and noble profession in sight, I had nothing but my good intentions. I would find out later that Jeanie was nursing her own doubts about me. As it turned out, it was the aunt with whom she was staying who convinced her to give me a chance:

"When Vincent and I met, I had already completed my nursing associate's degree and license, and was pursuing my bachelor's. For that reason, my friends, and most of my family, objected to the match. I suppose they were just being protective, but by and large most felt he was simply not good enough for me. One of my cousins—a doctor—weighed in on the matter too. 'No, no. He's not your type,' Doreen said, pointing out his lack of education and fashion sense. Other friends frowned at his home address. At the time he was living in the Bronx, which was quite rough in those days. So, after dating Vincent briefly, I broke it off. Soon after, however, my Auntie Mary asked me about 'that nice fellow' I used to date. When I told her I had ended it, she gave me a nurturing look. 'He seems like a gentleman, Jeanie,' she said in that manner of an older lady with the benefit of wisdom and foresight. 'I really think you should reconsider.'

"So, I thought back to the night Vincent and I met, and to our first conversation when he shared with me his plans for a business. I had to admit that there was something special about his quiet determination. It took me some time, but I eventually followed my aunt's advice."

Jeanie HoSang

After dating for a year or so, the pretty nurse decided to give the milkman with the GED a chance. We got married in a Long Island church on August 8, 1976, before about a hundred family and friends. I had just celebrated my thirty-sixth birthday just three days before. Scraping together enough money to take my bride on a Hawaiian and Las Vegas honeymoon, I threw myself at our island getaway and its candy-sweet pineapples. I loved them so much, in fact, that I returned to New York lugging a box, heavy with the delicious fruit. Weeks later, I discovered several places in the city that sold the Hawaiian-grown treat. It was yet another reminder that New York was a dreamer's paradise. There wasn't anything in this city that you couldn't get.

Jeanie and I began our life as a married couple on the east side of the Bronx in a three-room apartment rental that was part of a house. We had one bedroom, a full bathroom, kitchen, and living room. Life was immediately busy. I was still clocking in at the dairy company, while Jeanie continued her studies and worked at a daycare center. With our eye on our budget, we began looking for a small home to buy. When Jeanie became pregnant the following year with our first child, Damian, we put our savings together and bought a place on the northeast side—a legal three-family building with a basement that could be turned into another apartment. We took the second floor, leaving the ground and top floors for rental income. My friend Lynn took the ground floor, while another tenant took the top. With the tenants' rent offsetting our mortgage, we were eventually able to fix the basement and increase the property's value and rental potential. A friend of Jeanie's took the basement.

Now a man with a young family and growing responsibilities, I squinted at the immediate future. I was still doing well at Dairy Lea, but sensed that it was time to make another move. After Damian's birth, Jeanie continued studying for her bachelor's and took a job at North Central Bronx Hospital. Together we were putting food on the table and paying our bills. We were comfortable enough, but felt ready for more. As if reading my mind, my brother gave me a little push. "Maybe you should start looking for a business," King suggested. "If it doesn't work out, you can always return to what you're doing now. You're still young enough to correct any missteps. I'll help with a small loan if I can."

At about the same time, Jeanie began taking note of vacancies when we were driving. Eventually, she made the same suggestion. "Vincent, why don't we open a business of some kind? You've always wanted to do that, and I really think you should," she encouraged. I was relieved. Her nudge assured me that we had the basic ingredients in place for a chance at success. Now that I knew we were on the same page, I turned once again to a page of another kind—the business section of the *New York Post*.

Jeanie had suggested we focus on the areas with a strong Caribbean population. For months I combed the fine print looking for something suitable. I eventually replied to a couple advertisements that sounded promising, including one ad for a small restaurant on the west side of the Bronx. Deep down I had my reservations about another food retail business. I had not forgotten how my cousin and I were all but shackled to the restaurant we owned by the university back in Jamaica, but neither could I dismiss the profit potential of such a business. Done right, there was good money to be made in the food industry. The experience had at least taught me that much.

I got the call one December afternoon after a particularly grueling night at work. I had come home from my deliveries and fallen asleep only a few hours before. The phone, sitting inches from my ear, rang loudly. Jolted out of my slumber, I tried to wish it away. The problem was that I had this one strict rule I had yet to break: always answer the phone. "Hel-lo?" I answered, sounding every bit as groggy as I felt. There was a short pause followed by an upbeat male voice.

"Ah...oh! I'm looking for the person who called about the restaurant a few days ago?"

"Ye-es?" Looking back, I can only smile at the shaky first impression I must have made on my caller. I knew I wanted to make the big move. It was the reason I left my small pond to begin with, but I was still just a little terrified of wading out into the big deep, and possibly drowning. Still unsure, I took my last gulp of air before diving in. I sat up and started the conversation over again. "I mean, yes. This is Vincent. I'm the one who called."

"Well, hello then, Vincent. I'm Mike," the voice continued. "I own Kingsbridge Delights, the restaurant in the ad. If you're interested in seeing the place, then come on over and let's talk!"

I was there in half an hour.

Mike Ford was an Irishman with a firm handshake and broad smile. A retired fireman, he looked like he could handle any customer who had one too many at the adjoining bar he owned. That was, in fact, where we met.

Any reservations I had about the venture disappeared as soon as I met him. We hit it off instantly and sensed that we could do business together. Kingsbridge Delights was a small restaurant located on a main street, offering a basic menu of fried chicken, French fries, fish and chips, battered shrimp, and ribs. He had originally bought the business for his son who was completing his tour of duty in the navy. When his son returned, however, he told his father he wasn't interested in the restaurant. Left in the hands of a team of students he had hired, the restaurant, Mike admitted, was barely yielding a profit. He then added that if the place were owner-operated, the cash register had the potential to ring nonstop. He was sure of it. I knew he wasn't lying or exaggerating to make the sale. The fact that he had a profit at all was remarkable. On weekdays, the earliest they opened for business was 3:00 p.m.

When Mike showed me the restaurant, my eyes went everywhere like a pinball machine. The place was about 1,800 square feet, with flooring and walls that were screaming for attention. There were cracks, dents, and scrapes all over. I knew I would have to put some work into it first, but was not put off by the hurdle. Motivated to sell the business, Mike was asking for a ridiculously cheap rent. The issues were also purely cosmetic, and I had just the man to call for the renovations. Fred, the same English friend who had built my shelves for my bread depot and ice cream parlor in Kingston, had also left the small rock for the Big Apple. He could take care of the superficial blotches with one hand tied behind his back. Otherwise, the place had good bones and a winning location—it sat minutes away from a captive campus—the nearby VA hospital. After settling on a final price of $18,000 for the business, we put the paperwork in motion.

Meanwhile, some other paperwork I had set in motion the previous year was now coming through. On January 4, 1978, I finally became a citizen of the United States of America. As I stood there, my hand across my heart, I recited the pledge of allegiance before the flag. I felt as if I had just been taken in by an adoptive family. The match was a good one. We looked different, spoke with different accents, and even had different stories. Yet, in spite of it all, I knew we were looking at the future with the same hope for growth and prosperity.

After that day, I walked with a little extra steadiness in my stride.

CHAPTER 8

Fishing with the tides

"As a new New Yorker, I took note of the people who were behind the counters—the business owners. I noticed that many were immigrants like me, like my parents once were. Many came educated, and some with professions. Once they arrived on American soil, however, their fresh eyes saw something else: opportunity. Lots of it."

Vincent

THE YEAR WAS 1978. I WAS NOW A MARRIED MAN, A father, and a proud new American. A little over a month after becoming a citizen, I became an American business owner. I handed in my resignation at Dairy Lea the week I picked up the keys to the restaurant from Mike. I could hardly wait to floor the gas pedal of our new venture. In fact, I even arrived a tad late for the closing because I had first stopped at the bank to get change for the till—a couple hundred dollars' worth of coins. *Business was going to be great*, I told myself.

I spent the first week in training. Since my plan was to keep the same name and menu for the transition phase, Mike had his staff show us how to prepare everything. Still studying, now mothering, and also holding a full-time job, Jeanie was a trooper. She gave any spare time she had to the restaurant. It meant giving up her weekends and any real personal time for herself.

I still remember our sales for the first seven-day week we opened—it was an abysmal $960. My stomach sank into my shoes. There was no way we were going to pay our bills with that. I sucked back a deep breath. Even though I showed no signs of panic on the outside, a kernel of self-doubt tried to lodge itself in my mind. *Had I overestimated the restaurant's potential?*

Nervous but undaunted, I turned my attention back to the road before me and threw on the high beams. It was time to turn this around. Immediately, I diagnosed the most serious challenge choking the fledging business: quality control. There was practically none. If some of the fried chicken had been overcooked, for instance, the staff would sell it anyway. They even sold leftovers. I rolled up my sleeves and got to work.

"No," I said. "We can't have that. From now on we sell fresh only."

I then turned my attention to the ribs and to the six electric fryers in the kitchen. Two were for the fries, three for the chicken. The last one had something in it that looked like ten-year-old sludge. When I asked about it, the staff said that that was the fryer they used to heat the ribs. With no microwave available in those days, you either served fresh straight out of the oven, or reheated by dipping the ribs into hot oil.

I did not want to know how old that oil was. All I knew was that a spoon could have stood in it. Then, when one of the workers whispered that he had once been sick for three days after eating the ribs, I threw it right out. The way I saw it, there was only one choice: either go with quality or close our doors. "From now on we heat the ribs the right way," I said. "In the oven."

Day after day our sales inched up as the inches around my waist went down. I was constantly rubbing my eyes awake, but feeling good about the small wave of progress we were riding. It made crawling home at 11:00 p.m. each night worth it. I was just getting started, however. Curious about what volume a morning shift could bring, I decided to try opening at 7:00 a.m. We would keep it simple at first, I decided, and serve only coffee and muffins. I didn't know much about making coffee back then, only drinking it, but figured it looked simple enough.

Within days, word got around that we were now serving the breakfast crowd.

Patrons looking for a start to their day with a hot cup of brew began stopping by. Coffee, I realized, was a popular item in the cold climate, and so I kept the coffee service going all day.

One day, as evening approached, one of our regular customers came in and sat down. He was a tall, thin, slightly older Irishman, who ordered the same thing without fail: two fried chicken legs and French fries. He was so consistent that we would get the order going the second he walked in. This particular customer also liked to drink. We knew that because he usually smelled of stale sweat and fresh alcohol. The hot meal he had at our restaurant, we suspected, was his attempt to sober up.

That evening, a pot of coffee sat waiting as he walked in. It had been on the burner some two hours since the last coffee order. The gentleman, looking like he had indulged at the bar more than he usually did, ordered a cup. "Nice and hot, please," he said, going beyond his usual word limit.

Off I went to pour the dark brew. I noticed the change in smell, but didn't think anything of it. Less than a minute after serving it to him, however, I heard his voice. The fact that he was speaking was unusual enough. The fact that he was audible from a distance, was alarming. "Heeey!" he protested, trying to control his slur. "Whaddar ya giving me here? Muhd?"

Embarrassed, I flew to his table with an apology, a refund, and an offer to prepare a fresh pot. I figured that if a quiet drunk could muster the energy to complain, the stuff had to be pretty awful. That was the day I learned that coffee's shelf life on a burner is twenty minutes, and not a minute longer. I have not served a bad cup since. Today, I'm equally fussy about my cup of java. At my plant, my staff and I enjoy only premium grade every day, never burnt.

Always admit when you've made an error and make amends immediately. If your customers are reasonable, they will understand that mistakes happen. What they will not forgive is a cover-up.

I continued listening to our customers, and paid special attention to those who made it known that we were on a short leash—like the lady who came in one day and marched right up to the counter. "So. I guess you're the new owners?" she said with an air of mild impatience.

"We are," I said with a smile, wondering if I was looking at a new inspector of some sort. As it turned out, she was the most important kind of inspector yet—she was a discerning customer.

"Well, Mr. New Owner, let me have a three-piece fried chicken order to go. If you see me in here again, it means I enjoyed it. If you don't see me, well, you can figure out the rest." A few days later she returned. "Oh, so you're still here!" she said, her shoulders pulling back slightly.

"Yes, of course," I said, almost laughing. "Where should we be?" Then she finally relaxed into a smile.

"Well it's just that this restaurant has changed hands so often that I assumed…well, you know."

"I understand," I said smiling back. "Yes, we're here and ready to serve. What can we get you today?"

I made every effort to accommodate those who supported us. That included the customer who knocked on our door one night, fifteen minutes after we'd flipped over the *closed* sign. I had to think twice about opening that door, of course, as this was going to be either a legit customer or a holdup. I decided to chance that it was a customer. For him I opened the door, fired up the fryer, and made the nicest order of our fried chicken. He left happy with his twelve-piece bucket, side order of rolls, and cranberry sauce.

After six months of tweaking, we finally began to turn a sliver of profit. A busy weekend courtesy of the great Muhammad Ali helped push our numbers over that first tipping point. The Champ had been booked to fight at the armory across from the restaurant. We couldn't have asked for more. The sold-out event drew a massive crowd hungry for action and food. Everything we had for sale went out the door. There was not a dinner roll left.

We were now seeing just how strong the Caribbean population in the area really was. In fact, many of the nurses at the hospital were Jamaican, as were some of the students from nearby Lehman College. Once they got to know us better, the requests for Jamaican dishes began to pour in. Jeanie immediately saw the potential. I, on the other hand, was a little hesitant, having just come through six months of ironing out creases and wrinkles. Fortunately, she kept pushing me beyond my comfort zone. "We have the customers' attention," she rationalized. "If we don't strike now, we'll lose a golden opportunity to really impress them. If we don't grab it, someone else will."

I admit it. Procrastination was a secret struggle of mine then. It didn't help that I was not the natural-born cook that Jeanie was. My pragmatic wife, sensing her husband's hesitation, decided to take her suggestion from theoretical pondering to live test. She was right, of course. This was no time to be caught flat-footed. Not waiting for me to come around, she bought ten pounds of the best goat meat available, and took it to her Aunt Mary. "Auntie," she said, "please help me cook the best pot of curry goat anyone's ever tasted outside of Jamaica."

The curry goat went as quickly as we could cook it. From there, we added other homegrown favorites that had the power to make a homesick Jamaican weep. Not only did our Caribbean customers love the new menu, our Latino friends, curious to try the dishes that looked similar to their own, got adventurous. Before long they, too, were hooked. We had just had our first bite into a new market, thanks to Jeanie. We were ecstatic and craving seconds. With a one-year-old at home and our second child on the way, however, Jeanie could only do so much, so we hired a cook for the Caribbean dishes.

Once we felt comfortable with our core meals, we tweaked our product line and added a handful of treats from the island, like puddings and tarts. There was one savory treat in particular I knew had to make the cut—the Jamaican beef patty. For that I called on King. I had no experience making the traditional handheld pie. My brother flew up as soon as he could to show us how.

The restaurant was, among other things, a test of our physical fortitude. We were on our feet every minute of each day using our hands to make just about everything from scratch. I watched like a proud parent as our restaurant grew in size and stature. Mike was genuinely pleased that his former business was finally seeing its true potential. Others noticed as well. One day, while making his weekly delivery of chicken and beef to the restaurant, our meat vendor, a real down-to-earth guy by the name of Paul Oteri, took a look at the line of customers. "Man," he said nodding his head, his eyes wide with amazement, "Vin, one day you're gonna be so big I won't be able to supply you! I can see it already. Well done, my friend. Well done!"

The following year we took the restaurant to another level. Through an old friend, I met another Jamaican fellow by the name of Frankie. At the time, Frankie was working at a Bronx bakery on White Plains Road, about twenty minutes away. When he came to see me in my new restaurant with a mutual friend, Frankie took a quick scan at the patrons. I could almost hear his mind spinning while his eyes took in the scene before him. By the end of the visit, he was suggesting that I sell Jamaican hard dough bread. I listened with some interest, but didn't bite—at least not at first. "Bread? I dunno, Frankie. This is a restaurant," I said. "I don't see how bread could be a winner here. To make it worse, only Jamaicans know that particular bread." Thankfully, he pushed past my hesitation.

"Just try a half dozen. Can't hurt. At worst you'll have to eat bread for a couple weeks, and that may not be a bad thing." He waved in the direction of my sunken stomach. "You look like you could do with a few extra pounds."

"All right," I said, now curious about the test run. "Let me have a dozen."

I liked that this Frankie was adventurous enough to make the suggestion. I respected that. In the mind of a businessman, it's the untapped opportunity that gets the adrenaline flowing.

The following day at about noon, Frankie delivered twelve fresh loaves baked just hours before. I had to admit—the aroma alone made me want to tear into one. An hour after he left I was on the phone with him. The bread had barely touched the counter before they were heading through the door in customers' hands. I was never so happy to be so wrong. "Frankie," I said, "Can you guys supply me fresh bread on a daily basis?" It took all of a second for the roaring laughter to return from the other end of the phone.

"Sold out, huh?"

"Like winning lottery tickets."

"Won't say I told you," he said.

"Won't mind if you do as long as I can have your bread."

"No problem. Only thing is we can't deliver daily. We're too small for that kind of service."

"What's the best you can do?"

"Twice a week. Will that work?" I thought about it for all of two seconds.

"No. If we're going to sell bread it has to be made fresh daily, or not at all. Now that the bread has passed the test, I don't want to confuse our customers with sporadic service, so tell you what. I'll pick up my order myself on the days you can't deliver. Just have it ready so I can toss it in my car."

The hard dough bread was a hit. Day after day the pile of the fresh, dense bread disappeared from our window display like time-lapsed footage on fast forward. Meanwhile, sales on our other items remained strong. I confess to boosting those numbers by slipping under the United States Department of Agriculture's radar. We were quietly wholesaling a small amount of our patties in standard cake boxes. As we were selling insignificant quantities to only two small outlets, we managed to stay out of trouble. That said, I will still admit to breaking into a cold sweat each time I pulled up with those white unmarked boxes. I did not enjoy breaking the rules. I was not slapping myself on the back declaring our escape a "victory." All I wanted was a start, and was grateful for the nod of approval by our customers, Vincent's Deli on White Plains

Road and Cammock's on Eastchester Road. Both were among the first, if not *the* first, neighborhood grocery shops to cater to the Jamaican and Caribbean population in the boroughs. The foresight to target this growing sector made both entrepreneurs pioneers in their own right.

By this time, our first daughter, Sabrina, had been born. As a father, I regretted that I was not able to interact with my kids for more than a few hours each week. I consoled myself with the knowledge that the sacrifice was inevitably for them. *Our* sacrifice as a family was for us all.

> "It was not easy, those early years as a young family in a start-up business. It was hard work keeping our head above water financially while holding it together as a family. I pushed where I saw that Vincent was hesitant. When he went off blazing a trail, coming home late and exhausted, I gave him the space he needed. Patience, understanding and determination—that's what an entrepreneurial family needs to thrive."
>
> *Jeanie HoSang*

Thanks to Jeanie, we had won the approval of our niche market, and were busier than ever. One day, in the middle of our honeymoon period, we ran out of Scotch Bonnet pepper. A variety of chili pepper world-famous for its punishing heat, it adds a distinctive flavor that cannot be duplicated. Found mainly in the Caribbean, it is to Jamaican cuisine what salt is to others.

At the bakery we needed it, not just for our line of meals, but also for our patties. The bottom line was simple: no peppers, no business. I took a breath to keep panic at bay and forced myself into a solution-oriented mindset. I grabbed the phone and began calling every supplier I knew in the tristate area. Hours later I put the receiver down. Nothing.

Then it occurred to me that I could try my luck across another border. By this time, Toronto's Jamaican community had long taken root, and where there are Jamaicans, there are Jamaican patties. I knew of several outfits in that fine city enjoying strong patronage, including George's Tastee, Randy's Patties, Patty Palace, Non Nisa Patties, and Nicey's. Their patties were of such fine quality, even Jamaicans on the rock itself would find them hard to resist. I had remained old friends with a couple of these entrepreneurs, and knew I could call on them without hesitation.

On the occasion of my pepper crisis, however, it was to Allan Chin of Allan's Pastry Shop that I made my emergency call. Allan, who made a delicious handmade patty famous for its wonderfully flaky crust, was generally credited with being one of the first to introduce this savory treat to Torontonians. We had met sometime before through a cousin of mine. With our shared livelihood as our glue, we encouraged one another as entrepreneurs. While we didn't go as far as swapping recipes—there is, after all, a certain line one does not cross— we were still generous with suggestions. "Vinnie," he once offered, "if you're not using cayenne pepper in your patty, you might want to give it a try. It makes a difference."

"Allan," I told him on another occasion, "You could produce so much more volume if you used a Colborne machine. You should give it a try." It was a relaxed, open, and respectful bond between two industry players.

When Allan told me that Scotch Bonnet was readily available in his city, I had him order me ten cases. After we hung up, I began sorting out my schedule around the unexpected trip. I was grateful it was still summer. After a few minutes, I grabbed the phone and called another friend of mine to ask if he had any plans for the weekend. He confirmed that he was free. "Great!" I said. "Let's take a drive to Toronto."

We left before sunrise in my Oldsmobile. We arrived nine hours later to find Toronto enjoying a pleasant summer morning with a hint of crispness in the air—a sign that autumn was waiting impatiently. Once we got to Allan's, he set me up at a table so I could grind the peppers. I got down to the reason I had made the trek. While working, I spotted a fellow in the back making patties. He was moving as if his arms never knew fatigue. "Allan," I said. "What's the name of that impressive machine you have over there?"

He glanced up. "Ah, yes—that's Charles. He's one of our best people. Funny you should ask about him, he's moving to the States. Your neck of the woods, actually. I'm going to be sorry to lose him."

"I can see why," I said. I bounced my eyes between watching him work and watching my own hands on the grinder. "But why does he want to leave? Canada's a nice country. Does he know that it gets cold in New York too?"

"Yes," Allan laughed. "He loves it here but just feels that there are more opportunities for him in the States. Plus, he has a sister there, and family can be a strong pull. She's already filed for him. He's just waiting for his papers."

When I was finished working, I asked Allan to introduce us. I liked that this Charles wanted to do more with his life. I was impressed that he was willing to move from thought to action. As we shook hands, I got straight to the point and told him that if he wanted a job, I had one waiting for him. "Call and let me know when you're on your way to New York," I said. "If you decide you like working with us, I'll take care of you."

We returned to the States that same night with the precious Scotch Bonnet, and a potential deal for a new patty machine. I was back at work the next morning at 7:00 a.m. sharp.

CHAPTER 9

On the right track

"Give your business a chance to grow strong. Lean on it too early, and it may collapse under the weight. In my first business, I didn't draw a paycheck for the first six months. Even then, I only paid myself a hundred dollars a week."

Vincent

IT WAS NOW 1980, AND A LITTLE OVER TWO YEARS since we had bought the restaurant. Jumping hoops and ironing out the kinks had taught me a lot about doing business in America. More importantly, it confirmed that no amount of hard work could scare me. Well-meaning friends eyed me with concern about "all the pressure" I was putting myself under, but I'd always smile and assure them that I was fine. After all, without pressure, there can be no diamonds.

Part of that stress included several robbery attempts in the short time we'd been in business. One of the first happened after we had closed for the day. We were busy cleaning up, when the phone rang. Naturally, I answered it. The voice at the other end was male and aggressive. "You're still there," he said. "Good. Now, you're going to empty the cash register into a bag and drop it into the trash container around the corner." When he hung up, I called the cops.

Sometimes the thugs were kind enough to wait until we had left. One set got creative and broke in through the skylight in the middle of the night, but, as we had secured the cash before leaving, they didn't get away with much. It had not been an easy two years, but I was grateful for our progress. I was just recovering from the teething stage, when Frankie, who had become a good friend by this time, buzzed around once again with another winner of a suggestion. "Vin," he said sounding as if he'd just learned a great secret he couldn't wait to share. "I think you should put in a dough breaker. Do that and I'll come work for you."

"What do you mean?" I said looking at him. "So I can make bread? Like a bakery?"

"Exactly. All you're missing is the dough breaker. You already have everything else."

I had to admit that it sounded like a logical next step. We'd already proven that our customer base was ready for it, but space was the challenge. With every square inch jammed with the needs of the restaurant, I would have to be baking on the sidewalk.

I shelved the idea outwardly. Inside, however, a switch had been flipped. Thanks to Frankie, I was now thinking in terms of volume. It was, I believe, one of the first moments when I began to picture myself drilling into another level of business. *Could I really do it?* I told myself: *Absolutely.*

Months later, Frankie returned with another idea. By this time, he had left the first bakery to run a German bakery owned by a fellow from Montserrat. Richard, the bakery's new owner, had bought it as a going concern. The real concern, however, was that he was an absentee owner who was busy working in his own trade as a successful carpenter. "Vin," Frankie said as I took the bread from him and began stocking our shelves. "I'm positive that Richard would be open to selling the business. Why don't you approach him about taking it over? He's got way too much on his plate with his carpentry business as it is. The bakery is in a perfect location on a busy street."

"Exactly what kind of 'busy' do you mean?" I asked, still filling the shelves. The loaves felt soft and heavy, their tempting aroma seeping faintly through the bag. I pictured a pat of soft butter being spread over a thick—make that extra thick—slice.

"As in a shop-lined main street with a train station just across the intersection. That kind of 'busy.'"

I stopped what I was doing and looked at Frankie, his suggestion exploding in my head like Fourth of July fireworks. I tried to picture the location and the kind of beautiful, steady traffic that only a main street could generate. I knew he was coming to me with a bona fide deal. He would have taken it for himself, I think, had it not been for two factors that were significant enough to make him hesitate: he was a little older, and he had lost his only son in a tragic accident. For him, taking on the bakery would mean going it alone. It was generous and selfless of him to think of me. As exhausted as I was, I felt ready to graduate to something bigger. I craved progress. For me, it was comfort food to an empty belly. "If I took on this bakery, Frankie, are you saying you would stay and work for me? Because the only thing I know about baking is that there's flour involved." I knew I had heard his offer correctly the first time, but wanted to avoid any kind of misunderstandings.

He grinned and stuck a hand out. "I'll teach you whatever you need to know, boss."

I went to see the place the following morning before it was open to the public. It was still dark out, but that didn't stop me from seeing an incredible vision. Sunshine Bakery indeed had a golden location. Sitting on a wide main street, only yards away from a busy intersection, the bakery stared straight across the road at the Dyre Avenue train stop. I pictured customers rushing in to grab their fresh bread and treats on their way to work or home. In my head, I could hear that cash register ringing again and again.

Even though he had kept the original line of German pastries, Richard, the new owner, had successfully added Jamaican hard dough bread. It was an excellent litmus test. If that bread could do well here, other Jamaican baked goods could follow. There was enough of a Caribbean base to support it.

I decided that we were going to make this happen. It didn't take Richard and me long to hammer out an agreement we were both happy with. Before picking up my pen to sign, however, I asked him if the building's owners might be interested in selling. The question just flew out of my mouth. I didn't know whether or not I would even qualify for a loan, but, the rental income potential aside (the building included three ground-level stores), I just had to try for it. I had seen my father live under the thumb of a landlord and did not want to make the same mistake, not if I could help it. With this property's ideal location, I knew I couldn't miss.

When it comes to location, I believe that it is always better to go for a main street. You'll pay more, but you'll also get more.

As luck would have it, the owner was willing to entertain "reasonable offers" for the five-thousand-square-foot building. The owner, a friendly Italian lady approaching retirement, was now ready to liquidate her assets and live a little life. Her asking price was $75,000. I checked my financial temperature. All I could pay down was $20,000. I took a chance at rejection and asked her if she'd carry my mortgage. As if the heavens above opened up, she agreed. I would, on another occasion, buy property with "no money."

Once again, life reminded me that it had a wicked sense of humor. Not long after confirming the deal, Mike came to me with an unexpected offer. Because of some changes in his personal life, he was leaving New York for a new life in Missouri, and wanted to sell the entire building—all five units. He was determined that I should have it, and was giving me, his newest tenant, first right of refusal. His asking price of just over $100,000 was not unreasonable. As if to further heighten my agony, he was willing to take a deposit of only $25,000. My stomach twisted into an instant knot. "C'mon, Vin, think about it," he said, trying to persuade me. "I'll even give you a seller's mortgage. You need to own this place. You already own the restaurant, so you'd be a resident landlord. It's perfect! You can do this!"

I had my nose pressed against the window display of golden opportunity. Poor Mike was doing everything in his power to drop it into my shopping cart, but I simply didn't have the money. I had barely managed to scrape together the cash for the Dyre Avenue building.

For the first time in my life, I allowed fear to paralyze me. For days I talked to myself. Mike saw me struggle, and tried one last time to change my mind. I was touched by his faith in me. With the sick sting of regret already prickling all over my skin, I declined his generous offer with repeated apologies, telling him that I needed to focus on the fresh obligations I had just taken on. Even as I said the words, I knew I'd pay dearly for the decision. Soon after, a Jewish company scooped up the property for the asking price. As Mike wrapped up his New York City life and headed for Missouri, our new landlord increased our rent five-fold.

Today, that missed opportunity lives on as my first true business "what-if." I wish I had been more aggressive. I wish I had just walked into the bank and asked for a loan. That said, I still emerged a winner. The experience taught me an important lesson. I would never again let fear thwart a golden opportunity. Years later, Mike would look me up while visiting New York. We shared a good little laugh about the fine catch I had let slip through my rookie fingers.

Ignoring my wounds, I promptly returned my attention to Dyre Avenue, and completed the purchase of the building. Once it was mine, I bought the bakery. Richard and I shook hands and exchanged our sincere wishes for lots of luck and blessings. When we parted, he left looking pretty happy, as if he'd just caught the last train home.

I was a racehorse scratching at the gate.

I was now a forty-year-old man, a husband, father of two children, and owner of two businesses, plus some real estate.

Dealing first with management, I hired my brother-in-law to run the restaurant so I could focus on the bakery, whose name we had changed to *Royal Caribbean Bakery*.

The new name was a rallying cry intended to garner the attention and support of our real target market. While we would keep the German baker and continue that line of goods, the Caribbean diaspora was our main focus. Working seven days a week, we successfully added the Jamaican sweet treats to the line, including spice buns and bread. Of course, we also added the island's iconic fast food—the Jamaican patty. We had, by this time, massaged our recipe even further in the pursuit of patty perfection. If your eyes didn't roll back into your head at first bite, it wasn't good enough.

Looking like a cross between a turnover and giant empanada, *patty*, as Jamaicans call it, is a much-loved savory treat. Nothing about it is subtle. Its taste is as unique as the island's blend of colonial, East Indian and African heritages. On the inside sits a playfully piquant, incredibly juicy filling of ground beef, chicken, or vegetables. On the outside is the crust. Typically flaky, and a cross between yellow and orange, this dough-based envelope has been the subject of many a passionate debate. If ever there were a family secret recipe that goes to the grave, this would be it. Whether doughier, flakier, or in between, it is as personal as politics.

On its own, a patty can be a light meal on the go, or substantial snack. Sold on average for less than two dollars, what is often a poor man's meal in Jamaica still remains a favorite treat across all social classes there. No eyebrows arch in surprise to see a man sitting in his BMW, and holding the signature brown paper bag in his hand, his head hovering over its contents. One taste and you'll understand why.

Get your patty straight out of the oven, and the novice would be wise to proceed with respect. Bite too slowly, and the first burst of steam will grab your lips or cheeks before you can pull away. Bite too much, and the hot juicy meat comes spilling out of its pocket and onto your feet—and that could be a serious problem if you're barefoot.

After that first breaking of the crust, you use your fingers to push the pie up the paper bag from the bottom. With each mouthful, the tasty crust and exotic pungent spices blend in your mouth the way a favorite song sounds to your ear. Once at the end, your belly now warmer and heavier, you pop that final bit of dense crust into your mouth. You pause for a minute to wipe from your mouth and shoes the remnant flakes—a sign that you've just eaten a quality Jamaican patty. Then you take a minute to consider whether you have room for another.

No matter one's preference of bakery, one thing is certain: for a Jamaican, nothing makes the stomach go more single-minded than the aroma of a patty baking to perfection. As annoying as it is (because someone has to clean up the mess), the sight of the telltale golden flakes on the floor, table, or car seat brings a smile to the face—because that's what comfort foods do for the heart.

Even then, I had no idea what it was about to do for our lives.

CHAPTER 10

Do or Dyre

"Some say I've been lucky, but I believe I played an active role in 'finding' fortune. If I hadn't made certain sacrifices, I would not have been able to take advantage of those 'lucky breaks' when they appeared. So, I agree with those who see luck as something we make for ourselves. This should be a comfort to those who think that luck is a lottery."

Vincent

AS A KID, I USED TO HEAR THE EXPRESSION, "There's no road without corners; slow down before taking them." I used to assume the literal meaning, thinking that the adults were referring to the island's knotted roadways. Straight, smooth highways had not yet made it to the tropical paradise. Most of our roads had to wind, meander and crawl over and through steep hills and mountains. A few in particular were legendary and not for the fainthearted. One even bore the name *Mount Diablo*. As I grew older, I began to understand the real meaning behind the saying. I didn't know it then, of course, but the day I bought the bakery on Dyre Avenue was the day I was about to enter my first deep corner.

I was now a baker. Well, "apprentice" was more like it. By now, some of the watchful naysayers had begun to weigh in:

"Vincent's no baker."

"What does he think he's doing?"

"It won't work."

I took each comment with grace, and respectfully ignored them. Meanwhile, Frankie kept his word and walked me through baking boot camp. While I still couldn't bake terribly well by the end of my training, I had learned the mechanics, plus two important points: what controlled quality, and what affected cost—two things every business owner must know.

Driving myself on literally a few hours' sleep each night, I juggled the restaurant and the bakery, and trusted my team to do right by me when I had my back turned. By and large they were hard workers, with most happy to have a job, and eager to show it. Our first manager was a fellow by the name of Selburn Dacres. As he was married to Jeanie's aunt, Selly was family. He would work with us right up until his retirement, years later.

He, like the others in our small team, worked as if they had skin in the game. For that I was blessed.

Despite the help, however, I could feel the pressure building inside me. I had always been a quiet believer, but now found myself praying in the mornings at the first chance of some privacy. As we were still living in our apartment, the only place for that was the bathroom. It was a bit unorthodox, I'll admit, and I did worry about the irreverence of it all, but it was the best I could do. Each morning, after washing my face and patting it dry, I'd go down on one knee and close my eyes. In the few quiet minutes that followed, I would thank God for the blessings He had sent my way, and asked for His continued guidance. More than anything, I wanted to make sure that I was making the right choices. I had to make the best decisions, not just for my family and me, but also for our workers and their families. I couldn't let this domino fall.

Positive rituals are like daily supplements for the mind and soul. This simple gesture of quiet prayer—of meditating—became a treasured habit that helped to set my day's tone, and strengthen my resolve to soldier on.

My days rolled into a giant blur. They were not, however, without the occasional flashes of intrigue, like the day I learned that my new bakery had infamous connections to one of America's most haunting crimes—the Lindbergh kidnapping. I got the call early one day from the BBC producer in charge of the documentary. As it turned out, the kidnapper's girlfriend had worked at the same Dyre Avenue address when it was still the original German bakery, two owners before me. Naturally, I agreed to give the film crew full access to the premises. On the day of filming, however, they were met with disappointment. They had not anticipated that I had altered the interior. I'm not sure why it didn't come up in our conversation, to be frank. In the end, they shot footage of the bakery's exterior. It was brief, but it was free exposure nevertheless.

On another occasion, I had to face my own dance with extortion. It happened not long after we opened Royal Caribbean Bakery. I was in the kitchen helping with the baking, when a man came through the front door. Wearing a long-sleeve shirt and dark pants, he thundered in as if he owned the place, arms held slightly off his sides as if he was about to lift something. An older man with a slightly thick build, he looked like he'd seen some things in his time. When he asked to see the owner, I identified myself. "Hello, I'm Vincent," I said. "How can I help you, sir?"

He neither smiled nor frowned. Instead, he fixed his gaze on me and slowly placed his business card on the counter. When he began to speak, his speech was just as deliberate.

"Well, Vincent, I'm your 'assigned' sanitation service provider," he said with sarcasm as subtle as Scotch Bonnet pepper. "I just wanted to meet you in person, boss to boss, so that we can confirm our, ah, 'gentlemen's agreement'. You follow?"

With my gut telling me to remain silent, I nodded quietly as he advised me of his pick-up times and non-negotiable fee. A minute later, he was gone.

I had no proof, of course, but I'd have sworn that I had just been paid a visit by the mafia. I had heard about them since I arrived in New York, and knew that it was just a matter of time before I'd get trapped in its sticky web. I was the new kid on the block, still learning the rules of a playground notorious for its underground element.

Our uneasy relationship would come to an end a couple years later, much to my relief. Organized crime's grip on New York businesses was now being wrenched loose, thanks to the determination and courage of a then-young Rudolph Giuliani. With the ink barely dry on his 1983 appointment as U.S. Attorney for the Southern District of New York, Mr. Giuliani tackled New York's makeover with a fearlessness you couldn't help but respect. As a result of his efforts, those of us who risked our life savings to make a living in this great city could now relax our shoulders somewhat. It was all anyone could talk about. I decided that it was time for some cleaning up of my own.

One morning, when our "assigned" garbage collector was pulling up next to our container, I had one of the workers tell him to come see me first. I sat waiting behind my desk in my tiny office. I had no plan or strategy, except to terminate his services the same way it began—by making it clear that there was no room for negotiation. He came in a couple minutes later. "Well, my friend," I said, my eyes looking straight at him as if I knew something he didn't. I kept my fingertips on the table. "Thank you for your service. It's been great. But, as you know, times have, um…changed. Let's just say that things are… different now, you follow?" I said this, hoping he would read my attempt to invoke Giuliani's housecleaning effort. "So, we won't be needing you any longer." Looking a little taken aback, our sanitation man was the one to go silent. Seconds later, he nodded with a shrug, spun around, and left. That was the last I saw of him.

I would, some ten years later, miss the honor of thanking Mr. Giuliani in person for his outstanding work. I was delivering cocktail patties to the Gracie Mansion for an event he was hosting that evening as New York City's new mayor. Returning to my delivery van, I saw him in the distance talking with another gentleman. My first instinct was to walk up and introduce myself, but an old shyness flooded over. I would not let that opportunity escape me today.

Getting rid of our sanitation man did not end our rash of irritants, of course. We continued to be preyed upon by opportunists; some would-be, some successful, and some armed. A few tried to pose as customers who were unhappy with something they had bought from us. Their trick was simple: they'd appear minutes after closing, knock on the window, and point to a loaf of bread or bun in their hand. It worked only a couple times. No one was hurt, thank God, but the thieves managed to run off with the cash in the first instance, and the actual cash register with its contents in the second.

Then there were staff issues, like the case of the fellow I had hired from out of state. He had come to New York where he thought opportunities were better. To help him out, I set him up in a small apartment, and furnished it out of my own pocket. I even told him he could repay me slowly. One day, he had an accident at work. Unable to stay on, he left and returned to his family. Sometime after, I sent him a personal gift of some cash. To my shock, he took that money and tried to sue us. As our workman's compensation insurance covered his medical expenses, however, the only thing the lawsuit satisfied was his lawyer's pocket.

A similar incident happened with another worker. He was, in fact, one of our managers at Dyre. I also went out of my way to help him with a place to live, even going as far as to co-sign a loan for furniture. One day, while he was still in our employ, I got the call from the bank saying that he had stopped servicing the loan.

Then, there was the case of the driver with selective hearing. In his job interview, I told him what the benefits were, and specified that paid sick leave was not one of them. There was only so much we could afford as a start-up company. Eventually, however, he took ill. When he returned a week later, I told him we would pay him for half the week, even though we were not obligated to. He said nothing, and went to stand by the van while it was being loaded. Once it was full, he sent word that I could call him when I was ready to pay him for the rest of the week. With that, he left. I never did call him back.

I wince when I hear someone knocking his or her boss or employer. The way I see it (acts of abuse notwithstanding), if you find your situation that unbearable, it's better to leave and find something more suitable than to stay and complain. Once you've accepted a job, you must work with heart. This is especially true when working in your family's business. I believe that family should work harder, and not indulge in liberties. I will never forget the young Korean girl who worked at her family's dry cleaning business in my neighborhood. She was behind the counter having lunch the day I walked in. Smiling, she put her plate down and greeted me. Even now, I will answer the phone if the switchboard is busy. I'll take care of my customers mid-meal if I must. The food can wait. The customer cannot. A business without superior service is a product with a short shelf life. It won't last.

For all the disappointments we endured, however, I enjoyed the uplifting moments that kept cynicism at bay, moments that showed me the true value of my journey. Like the time a customer asked for advice on how to set up and run a business like mine. I told her everything: where to buy the equipment, how to cost her products, what sells, what doesn't, how to organize the workflow for optimum efficiency, and the importance of location.

When considering a food retail business, particularly an ethnic one, look at the neighborhood. It's important that it be somewhat receptive to your product. That initial revenue stream is critical. Don't make the classic mistake of jumping in completely. Also, when carrying out your due diligence, consider your research source. I learned this during my milkman days, when thinking of options for the future. While on my Bronx route, one day, I asked one of my customers if she thought the Jamaican beef patty would do well there. She was a friendly lady who had taken a liking to me, so I felt sure that she'd be honest in her assessment. Her reply was an immediate "no." The hitch was that she didn't realize there was a growing Caribbean population in the area. Lesson learned: ask the wrong people and you'll get the wrong answer.

Another tip I passed on to my inquiring customer was the importance of paying one's bills on time. I had always made my bills my priority. It wasn't that I enjoyed parting with my money, but I was not the kind of person who denied another his money for sport. That may thrill some, but, for me, prompt payment was—and still is—a matter of common decency. I also reminded her that it's the happy supplier who will cut you some slack when you really need it.

I told the would-be entrepreneur all this and more. Not only did she end up with a successful business, she would eventually live out her retirement in sunny Florida. I enjoyed many such opportunities to share my business knowledge with others. I was humbled by each request for advice, grateful for the chance to give to them what had been given to me along the way.

The real joy came, however, when I saw the correlation between our financial success and our ability to help individuals in real distress. Such was the case of the lady on the verge of homelessness after a series of missteps. I learned about her plight one morning while reading a small feature on her in the community newspaper. With no hope in sight, she faced certain eviction from her apartment. Immediately, I thought of my father and how a small network of family and friends had saved us from the streets.

That week, I made contact with the minister in her area, and arranged to clear her arrears. I was still carrying a mortgage, and still had to watch our cash flow, but I knew we could find a way to help. I wanted to send her the message that she should always have faith. More than anything, I wanted her to know that someone in that vast city cared. I will never forget the look of shock and gratitude in her eyes when we met. For me, it was like seeing the lights on a magnificent Christmas tree lit for the first time. Not only did it fill my soul with purpose, it gave me an even stronger drive to be successful.

After that first experience, I kept going. Sometimes I'd be the one to initiate the offer of help. In other cases, the individuals in a pickle approached me. In the beginning, I almost always obliged. Unfortunately, as time went on, a few shady characters took me for a ride. One was a pastor. He was one of several within our community we had befriended, and even invited to our home on occasion. So, when he came to me with his hard-luck story a few months later, I didn't hesitate to reach into my pocket for a soft loan. He thanked me repeatedly, and showered me with prayers for God's protection. Not long after, he skipped town.

While I still feel privileged for being able to help those in need, I have since shed some of my naivety when it comes to philanthropy. I learned that, sometimes, people create their own chaos. They get into trouble because they didn't have the courage to sacrifice as we did. Today, when I sense that I am faced with such a situation, I find the courage to say "no."

Now well into my seventies, I still hesitate to turn anyone away. Helping others out of a jam puts a lift in my step. It fills my purpose bucket. I know in my heart that this is the main reason God has guided me in this direction, but you can only help the person who understands why they faltered. Otherwise, you're merely throwing away good money after bad. Today, I reserve my soft spot for two kinds of individuals: those who show true initiative in helping themselves, and those who are so badly off, they literally cannot try. I'm thankful that my radar is better at picking up the career opportunists. I'm sure God is relieved too.

Our beef patties were flying out of our bakery like the latest scandal. New vendors approached us about wholesaling our patties. One fellow came from out of the blue and said he'd buy them, but for a reduced price. We could even use less meat if we wanted to, he offered, but I politely declined.

It was clear that the time had come for us to take our product to the next level. It was a bittersweet challenge. With all my funds swallowed up by the purchase of the bakery, I didn't have enough left for the repairs and changes needed to meet USDA approval. The law spoke clearly on this matter: no USDA stamp, no wholesaling of meat or chicken products.

I attribute the demand for our products to two reasons. For one, our patty tasted pretty good. It had to. Our customers were, and still are, the kind who will let you know when you've disappointed them. Two, at the time we were one of only two Caribbean bakeries in the five boroughs that could produce in any kind of volume. With the Caribbean-American population growing rapidly, we had positioned ourselves as one of the new players ready to serve a captive market.

I stuck my finger in the wind to check the forecast. Two significant systems were about to converge: the sum total of all our hard work, and the opportunity we'd been waiting for. Inside, I allowed myself a small smile.

CHAPTER 11

Perseverance, perseverance, perseverance

"There's a reason New York is the gold standard by which to judge one's ability to survive. Competition here is that fierce. But with over eight million residents from which to build your customer base, I often wonder if the opposite couldn't also be true: If you can't make it *here*, then you can't make it *anywhere*."

Vincent

WE WERE STILL RUNNING TWO BUSINESSES: THE restaurant and bakery. By now it was clear that our Jamaican patty was our emerging rock star. Sales for that one item had sailed way ahead of our other products. Without hesitating, we tucked in behind its wake and adjusted our course.

When we first began producing the pies at the restaurant, we were making them with a single hand-operated contraption with a feeder and well—your basic turnover maker. It was a simple but painstakingly slow process. After making the dough from scratch, we would pre-sheet it in batches, cut them to seven-inch by six-inch pieces, put one piece of dough in the cavity, fill the well with a spoonful of the beef filling, then crank the handle until the dough enveloped the filling to become a half-moon-shaped pie crimped at the edge. That produced one unbaked beef patty. Our best was a hundred a day. Today, that first-generation gadget sits like a treasured keepsake on a shelf in our Tappan plant, far away from the boisterous energy of its massive modern-day replacement. I often walk past it as I go about my day. It reminds me how far we've come.

Once at Dyre, I added a couple more of those hand-operated turnover makers. Soon, we were in the big leagues with a whopping five going at one time, all day long. While we worked at a good clip, it was our mixer that actually limited our speed. The most it could take at a time was thirty pounds of flour. I knew I needed to ratchet up production if we wanted to take the leadership position in the market.

My mind spun as I made dough with my team, batch after batch. *There has got to be a better way. There has to be some kind of machine for this.* I began the hunt. There was, of course, no such thing as a Jamaican patty machine. It was just a matter of finding something that came close enough, requiring only a few minor modifications.

I soon found one semi-automated machine I felt had potential. In its bid to convince us that we were correct, the manufacturer confirmed that it had sold the same machine to another customer producing the same product. However, paying that particular customer a visit was not an option—no one was allowed into its factory, least of all, a competitor. I wasn't surprised.

Fortunately, the machine purveyor was a motivated one. If we brought our raw material to them, they said, they'd demonstrate its capability right there on the floor. We took them up on their offer.

While sorting out the final delivery and installation details, the company's engineer told me a story he thought I might derive some benefit from. He had sold the same piece to another company years before, and offered the guarantee of a refund if the machine failed. Not long after installing it, he received a call from the customer—the dough was sticking to the machine. They wanted to return it.

Unhappy, but willing to honor his word, the engineer arrived at the customer's plant at the end of the day, just as production was over. The only person in the room was the cleaning lady. She nodded quietly in his direction and continued briskly sweeping the floor as he approached the faulty machine.

As he began dismantling it, however, he heard a small voice behind him.

"Mister? Mister, what you doing?" It was the cleaning lady. Older and speaking slowly with a strong German accent, she eyed him suspiciously, the broom still in her hand.

"Oh, ah, your boss is returning this machine," he replied.

"But why? What wrong wiz machine?" she asked, her eyes narrowing.

"The dough seems to be sticking to the die."

"Dat is it? Dat is all za trouble?"

"Well, yes," the engineer replied, amused at her persistent interest. "Seems to be!" She gave him a look of mild annoyance.

"Well what about you add heat? Heat fix problem. You try. You see."

At that point the engineer stopped what he was doing. He stared at her in a moment of disbelief as he processed her suggestion. Seconds later, he was bolting out of the room to find the customer.

"Please," he said, "Let me try one more thing before I pull this down."

He found a blowtorch, applied the heat as the little old lady suggested, and ran some dough through it. Sure enough, the dough came out, clean as a whistle. In fact, it was perfect. The lady gave a satisfied "I-told-you-so" nod, and got back to sweeping the floor. Now smiling, the customer told the engineer that he'd be keeping the machine after all.

The engineer laughed openly with a shaking of the head as he finished the story. He would never forget, he said, the day a little old cleaning lady showed him, the young hotshot university-degreed engineer, how to clean up a sticky situation.

There is genius in everyone. It doesn't matter where you fall on the company hierarchy, or how little formal education you have. I always turn to my workers when looking for a better way to do something. They're the ones doing the work every day. They will see things I may not.

I had invested thought in selecting the right people to join our team. One of my new right-hand men was my old friend Lynn. He didn't hesitate to join us, even when I warned him that we were working nonstop. A saint disguised as a man, Lynn was the one who stayed back with me in the evenings to carefully measure out our seasonings for the following day. He, too, worked with the heart of an owner. For his friendship, loyalty, and dedication, I will always hold him in the highest regard.

I disappeared into my long days, resigned to peeking in at my sleeping children when I finally crawled home. By this time, we had, not two, but three young ones. Simone joined our family in 1981, a year after we bought the bakery. With three children under the age of five, Jeanie had her hands full. We let the division of duties unfold naturally in a way that worked best for us—she took care of the children while I took care of the business. With the help of the German line baker, I was able to spend half days on Sundays relaxing with my family. When the weather was nice enough, Jeanie and I would take the kids to Mohansic State Park (now the Franklin D. Roosevelt State Park) for a picnic lunch and some boating. The half days were hardly enough, but it was all the free time I had. All I could hope for was that our children grew up seeing the life I was building for them, even if it meant seeing less of me. I was determined that they not have even a small taste of the poverty that had been my childhood.

Naturally, I didn't have much time for socializing at this stage of my life. Through the business, however, I was lucky enough to meet a few genuine souls who became, not just acquaintances, but the kind of friends you can call at 2:00 a.m. with an emergency:

> "I first met Vincent in 1981 when I was an agent with New York Life Insurance. I somehow got his name, and made like Dick Tracy to track him down. I did that with every prospective client.
>
> "We spoke on the phone a few times. He was always good about taking calls, but no matter what I did, I could not pin him down for an appointment. From his tone, I could tell that he was a busy man, and not ready for my products. But something about him told me to keep the

channels open. One morning, I took a chance and popped by his bakery.

"I walked in, attired in my suit, briefcase in my hand. There, at the top of a ladder, was a man in basic slacks and polo shirt peering through what looked to be a vent of some kind. I had no clue what Vincent looked like, but assumed that this had to be him. Only a business owner could look this interested in a dusty crater in the wall. I was immediately struck by how hands-on he was. There was no shortage of workers around, so he could have easily had one of his people do the grunt work. 'Hi, Mr. HoSang!' I chimed, giving him my widest smile. Still on the ladder, he returned the smile before climbing down. After gripping my hand in a firm handshake, he immediately offered me a cold soda and something to eat.

"My first impression of him was of a man with hands full, and mind racing in high gear. That I had come at a bad time was patently obvious, yet he showed neither annoyance nor impatience. He appeared then as he does today—impossibly unpretentious, incredibly sincere, and friendly in a confident but understated way. We chatted for a few minutes before I thanked him for his time. I left without scoring his business that day.

It didn't matter. I had gained just from having met him. I did not know it then, but phase two of our association would come several years later."

Aston Lue

Fellow Entrepreneur

Relief to my hectic life came in 1982 when we sold the restaurant. I felt the collar around my neck loosen as I turned all my attention on the bakery. Every day I watched as the cash register bloated with cash, which happened several times a day on occasion. At Easter—a popular time for fruit bun—sales intensified, forcing us to empty the till almost every half hour. I had to force the smile off my face.

I'll never forget one Easter in particular, the year we had Dyre Avenue choking on traffic. It was Holy Thursday evening. Customers, anxious to grab their fresh-baked bun, were triple-parked outside the bakery. The crowd soon attracted the attention of the police, who came in wanting to know what the riot was all about.

The bakery was always buzzing with action, much to the frustration of customers who drove there. I met one such distressed customer early one morning as I was walking in. He had come by early deliberately, he said, because he was tired of getting tickets while picking up his bread. His story inspired one of our more memorable radio commercials, which we still affectionately call the "Pink BMW commercial." A friend helped tweak the script so that it flowed just right. It tells the story of a customer who double-parks her pink BMW in front of the bakery. Just as she's about to pay the cashier for her delicious fresh-out-of-the-oven Jamaican patties, another customer sticks his head through the front door in a panic:

"Does anyone here own a pink BMW?" he bellows.

"Yes! Me!" she says. "Whappen'?" (Jamaican for: "What's happening?")

"Well the meter maid is about to slap a ticket on your car!"

"Oh no," the customer whines, "I *knew* this was going to happen, but I am *not* leaving without my patties! Ah radda get di ticket. A'm coming all di way from Brooklyn!"

For the year during which it aired on the Gil Bailey Show, our Pink BMW commercial was voted number one. I still laugh when I think back to those days when I was still very much the "new kid" learning on the job. This was especially true when it came to marketing and advertising. The only thing I knew was that there was a whole world out there waiting for our products. We just needed to let them know who we were, where we were, and what we could do for them. As this was New York, however, the need for real exposure came quickly. A friend mentioned to me that she knew the right person to call:

"I got the call from Vincent after a mutual friend slipped me his name. At the time, I was working with WLIB radio station, the only game in town as far as Caribbean programming in the tristate area was concerned. If you wanted to reach that diaspora, WLIB was your 'channel.'

"The first thing Vinnie said was that he'd heard good things about me. 'Conroy, I'm expecting only the best from you,' he said, giving me an instant vote of confidence. I could tell he was smiling. Three or four days later, we met in person. From his body language alone, I sensed his humility. His handshake and smile put me at ease right away, and sealed for me what was already an indelible first impression. We discussed plans for an advertising campaign.

"As we talked further, he shared the story of his childhood without any prompting. As I listened, I got the impression that here was an individual who had known rough times, who wasn't afraid to work, and who was prepared to give what success demanded. In fact, I got the distinct impression that he used those memories the way athletes today use energy drinks. That day, I left his company knowing that I had just met a man programmed for success. I could not have guessed how right I was.

"Over the weeks, months, and years that followed, that certainty multiplied as his popularity in the community began to grow. His name was now out there—not just as a successful businessman, but also as a philanthropist. Yet, even as he became successful, Vincent continued to be a fixture at the workplace. In that regard, he is like others who build their businesses block by block.

"As our interaction increased, I had the opportunity to observe him as a boss. I saw him lean more on the mentoring side, and less on the hardnosed. It's not that he doesn't expect you to perform—he does—but he makes it clear to his workers that he sees them. I remember once being in his office when an employee came to him with a problem. The fellow stood at the doorway and glanced with hesitation at me. Vincent waved him in. 'Don't worry about Conroy. You can say anything in front of him!' After the fellow explained the issue at hand, his boss assured him, with the tone of a father, that they'd work it out.

> "I left WLIB in 2003. By that time, Vincent's enterprise had grown to become one of the largest manufacturers of patties and Caribbean food products in the United States, if not the world. Those of us in the advertising fraternity who were there from his early days, still marvel at this quiet giant's journey."
>
> *Conroy Allison*
> *Broadcaster, Winner's Circle Radio*

We continued to give Conroy our advertising business after he left WLIB. I made it a hobby to "collect" for my arsenal genuine people who were also competent professionals. I did this, not just because they were good at their job, but because they were also good company. I never fake a friendship for false motives. Using people is just bad business.

Another great person whom I had grown to respect was a gentleman by the name of Jeff Barnes:

> "Vincent is the perfect example of a no-excuses kind of individual. That man arrived in this country poor, but did what Jimmy Cliff told us to do: try and try. I think that's why he has a particular rapport with those who are struggling to make it on their own. He's walked in their shoes.
>
> "When Vincent started advertising back in the day, I was studying for my law degree and hosting a weekend show on WLIB radio, where I'd been since 1981. When I started practicing law, I stayed on. Meanwhile, as his business grew, his advertising with us increased.
>
> "From the start, he was the kind of person you could count on. Not only did he become one of the show's biggest sponsors, he supported us in other ways. If a promoter was having an event— let's say a dance or festival—Vincent would let us sell tickets at his bakery. On my radio program, I had a segment called 'Positive Personality,' showcasing community members who had made great achievements. Vincent agreed to be one of my first guests. He was always willing to help out, no

matter how busy he was. That's Vincent, though. If he can help, he will. He deals with everyone at this level—it doesn't matter who you are.

"In 1994, I was unexpectedly fired from the station. It shocked many, including Vincent. When I moved to another radio station, he went with me without hesitation. I can't explain what his support and loyalty meant, even today.

"What I admire most about him, however, is that he doesn't stand still. He's always working toward the next goal. That said, when he opened the Tappan plant, it stopped even me in *my* tracks. Up to that point, I had never seen a Jamaican achieve in *this* country on *that* scale. As he gave a group of us a tour, he had this look about him. It wasn't self-importance. It was happy confidence.

"His name is now synonymous with Jamaican patties, but if you ask me, I think his community outreach is his real mark. He was born with congenital kindness. That's why I tell people all the time, if I make it to heaven, my first question will be: 'Where is Vincent HoSang?' Wherever he is, that's the corner I want to be in."

Jefferyson A. Barnes, Esq.

Between our product tweaking and advertising, we were, at long last, seeing a profit. Our new success, however, came with an interesting challenge—space. With production inching up steadily, the 2,500-square-foot outfit we had moved into was beginning to feel snug at the waist. No matter how hard I looked, I could find no room to expand. I kept my mind open for a solution.

A year later in 1983, my friend Allan called from Toronto. Charles' papers had finally come through. He would arrive in New York within the week:

> "The day Vincent made me a job offer in Toronto, he came across as the real deal. He looked me in the eye, not up and down like he's trying to decide what I'm all about and that kind of thing. Just to be sure, though, I asked my old boss about him. When Allan assured me that Vincent would do right by me, I relaxed.
>
> "I arrived in New York in November. When I went to the bakery, I met Frankie, who told me that Mr. HoSang was not in. When I mentioned that I was there for 'the job,' he looked surprised and said that they weren't hiring, so I left. The next day, Vincent, who had been expecting me, asked if anyone had heard from me. When Frankie told him what had happened, Vincent jumped. 'What?

No! Call him back! That's the new Jamaican patty machine from Toronto I told you about!'

"That was over thirty years ago. Since then, he's kept his word and has helped me personally many times—with my car, my mortgage, you name it. In fact, he was the one who bought me the first bed I owned in New York. He's just a super person, and not just with me. No one here is afraid to go to him with problems. He's like a father here, especially with the female staff. He speaks to them with kindness and respect. He's always teaching them about saving money. It's his 'thing.' I once overheard him explain that it's not how much you make, but how much you save. You can make a million dollars a year, he said, but if you spend a million and one dollars, then you're poorer than the man who makes thirty thousand a year but saves one hundred.

"As a boss you can't get any better. In all my time knowing this man—and I see him almost daily—I have never heard him swear, slam a door, or raise his voice. If something is really bothering him, you might know it because you see a little tension in his eyes. But to take his mood out on others? Never. He may talk with some 'urgency' in his tone if he can't get his product out—and that is to be expected from any business owner.

But with him, there's no drama, not even when you'd expect it. There was a tunnel oven fire once in our main line. Even while standing before a fire, our boss remained calm. All he wanted to know was that we were all safe. That instilled incredible confidence in us—that's the sign of a true leader.

"As a manufacturer, he deserves complete respect. His first ingredient is quality. The word *shortcut* is not in his vocabulary. For instance, I remember once getting a delivery of beef with a shorter than usual expiration date, so he returned it to the vendor. As a business owner, he's so hands-on, you'd think he's forgotten that he has a staff. We've all seen him cleaning the bathrooms—not just his but the general one too. He'll mop floors and wipe down machines. If someone's moving something heavy, he's there. We'll tease him. 'Now *why* are you doing that, Mr. HoSang?' Or, 'Why don't you take a longer vacation this time instead of the usual few days?' He'll just laugh and give us the same answer—that he can't sit still. This plant is his home. He knows every square inch, every machine, every step of the process. If there's a work challenge you're trying to overcome, he stays with you because it's *his* issue. He doesn't abandon you just because he's paying you to deal with it. He's that protective. Not surprisingly, he's had little practice at firing. I'm usually the one to say, 'Look, Vincent, so and so has gots to go, man.' Without fail he'd be buzzing in my ear begging me to reconsider. He's all about that second chance.

"I've learned a lot from him. He has this way of explaining things so they stay with you. I remember once running out of thyme, one of our key ingredients for our patties. We couldn't get our order delivered for some reason, so Vincent asked me to go with him to pick it up. Now, it just so happened that he had just bought his first luxury car—a gorgeous Mercedes Benz. So I asked him if he was really going to abuse his sweet new ride with pungent thyme. That's when he turned to me with that signature grin of his, the one that signals that he's about to school you. 'Charles,' he said, 'it's the thyme that bought the Mercedes.'"

Charles Chung
Production Manager
Caribbean Food Delights

By now, it was baked in my mind that our patty was our future. Unable to find an unused square inch in the bakery, we were forced to store the baking racks in the customer serving area at nights so that we could clean the kitchen floor. That meant pulling the racks out on the sidewalk in the morning to access the bakery. We were in the position every business owner dreams of—we had more demand than product. If we didn't grab the attention now, we'd lose it in a New York minute. In my mind, there was only one clear solution—a bigger place. I had to pinch myself in a fleeting moment of disbelief. We had only just gotten here.

As the adrenaline flooded my veins, my mind ran on the passenger who had helped me out with the beer. New York was living up to his warning. It had not been the easiest nut to crack. Yes, we were now enjoying a modest banquet, but there had been many times when I swallowed lumps of fear down my constricting throat.

There is an upside to sticking to such a diet, however—eventually, you develop a taste for courage.

CHAPTER 12

The climb steepens

"Whether in your personal life, job, or business, don't waste your time, energy and talent on derailing your competition. Keep your eyes forward and focus on *your* goals, on *your* best effort. Even a quick glance back could cost you the grand prize."

Vincent

WE HAD SOLD OUR RESTAURANT IN 1982, CONTIN-
ued running our new bakery on Dyre Avenue, taken our first steps at formal advertising, and were now planning our future around our Jamaican patties. Our business vitals were spot on. I felt as if my days were blessed with blue skies and a steady

wind at our back. The only thing keeping production from soaring was space.

Fortunately, by this time I had already brought into the fold a sharp and seasoned architect by the name of David Cybul, of then Cybul & Cybul Architects. Backed by a talented team that included his son, Martin, it was David who confirmed that I was on the right track.

"This place is too small to be USDA compliant," he said. "If that's what you really want, Vincent, there's nothing else to do but find a bigger location."

While I had always felt that luck was something we made, I concede that there are times when one is indeed blessed with it. David Cybul was one of those blessings. A Jewish American some fifteen years my senior, he quickly became my business associate and friend. Before long, our discussions went beyond the matters of factory layouts, blueprints, and expansion details. David, perhaps sensing that here was a new immigrant who needed a little guidance during the acclimation process, seemed to instinctively cast a protective eye on me. So, it was no surprise to anyone when I asked the Yale graduate and registered member of the American Institute of Architecture to sit on our board of directors. This singularly decent man and loyal friend would remain a fixture at Caribbean Food Delights until his passing in 2013 at the age of eighty-nine. It was, for me, a personal loss. I still miss his faithful counsel, but today have the honor of working with his equally talented son. Armed with a BA in architecture from Tulane University and no less than two masters' degrees from MIT—architecture and systems engineering—Martin Cybul made his father beyond proud:

"Growing up, I'd hear Vincent call my father 'Uncle.' The moniker was an appropriate one. Dad loved Vincent and took on the role of godfather, giving him consistently sound advice where his business was concerned. It was not unusual for Dad to 'adopt' certain clients, but he seemed closest to Vincent. They were something of kindred spirits. Both were immigrants who'd been shaped by tough times. Men of vision, they were particularly matched in their approach to projects. It was always about quality. They believed in doing things properly, with longevity in mind. It meant cutting out the shortcuts. That made a client like Vincent an architect's dream.

"My father was what is called a *Sabra*—a Jewish term meaning *tough on the outside but soft on the inside*. Born in Palestine before it became Israel, David Cybul was a product of the Great Depression and then the Greatest Generation, having served in the United States Navy as a lieutenant during World War II. He then began the next phase of his life by going to Yale and getting his bachelor of architecture. These events molded him. As a result, he had this tendency to be protective of someone like Vincent, who is basically sweet and, oftentimes, too conciliatory. By virtue of his own personality, others would readily take advantage of him. That incensed my dad, who would then go to battle for his friend.

"Despite Vincent's trusting demeanor, my father had every confidence in him as a businessman. To his credit, Vincent came into a highly competitive industry and built it from the ground up at a time when others could not. I've been watching his rise to success since 1979, when I began working with my father. I admit that we could not have anticipated Vincent's success—from a small store on Dyre Avenue, to his present compound at Tappan. That said, I am also not surprised. Knowing him as I do today, I can say that his drive to succeed comes from a place deep within. It comes from wanting to serve his family and those who are struggling. That, more than anything else, is his true legacy."

Martin Cybul, RA, AI
Partner, Cybul Cybul
Wilhelm Architects

The image of a bigger bakery now in my plans, I kept my eyes open for something suitable. Meanwhile, the square footage in our home was also taking a big squeeze. With the birth of our last child, Brian, in 1983, there were now six of us in our apartment. Space wasn't the real concern, however. That was temporary. It was time—time with my family. Building a business while raising a young family is not always the ideal, but I did my best. Sometimes it meant combining both:

"When Damian and I were old enough, Dad would take us to the bakery on Sundays to help him count money and make sure everything was ready for the following day. I can't say that I woke up happy to go. We had to get up really early. So early, in fact, it was usually still dark and deserted by the time we got there. The first thing Dad did before getting out of the car was to look around for troublemakers. He'd be just as vigilant as he unlocked the padlock. Then, when he flew the shutters up, I'd clasp my hands over my ears to block out the horrific roar.

"Once we were safe inside and the door was bolted, I'd run to the light switches and flip them on, just as he had taught me. That was my little job. To warm us all up, he'd make Damian and me hot chocolate, and him coffee. Damian and I would sit patiently in our chairs waiting. Once the first sip of that hot liquid velvet hit my tummy, I'd smile and swing my legs about the chair.

"After that, he'd get us on counting the money while he took care of other things. You'd think that counting was straightforward, but he had a system for it. 'Don't go one, two, three,' he'd say, 'Go two, four, six, and so on to make it faster.' That was Dad, always trying to teach us something useful, and always with incredible patience. Whether it was math homework or anything else, he'd show you a hundred times in a row if you wanted. He'd never fuss or complain, no matter how tired he was.

"The lessons continued at home too. A big discipline trigger for him was the wasting of *anything*. If we were brushing our teeth, he'd remind us to close the faucet until we were ready to rinse. If we left a room, we had to turn the lights off. And food—you had to eat what was on your plate. I once missed the ice cream truck because of a couple mouthfuls of black-eyed peas. The rule was we could go play once we'd finished our dinner. So when I heard the truck's familiar song approaching, I chewed faster. The problem was I didn't like black-eyed peas and just couldn't swallow them fast enough. The rules were the rules, however. That day, there would be no ice cream for me."

While we were adjusting to the rhythm of owning a family business, the dynamics at the bakery had also changed. As if overnight, not only did the customers know us, so did the sanitation department inspectors. They knew our name well, spelling it correctly each time they cited us for our violations. Our most frequent infraction was the "storage" of the racks on the sidewalk in the mornings. *You don't own the sidewalk*, we were told. It was a fact we could not refute. We paid a fine of $50 each time we were caught.

I would soon find out sometime after that we were now featured heavily on the radar of certain other parties. My hunches were confirmed during yet another Easter season. It was Holy Thursday. I went in earlier than usual that morning to join the workers for a long day of baking. It was still dark when I parked my car on Dyre. The only thing I could see clearly was whatever sat directly under the street lamps. Sitting in the shadows in a parked sedan were two men. I caught them out of the corner of my eye, and wondered if I was about to be held up again.

When they entered the store minutes later, I was behind the counter. Walking in with purpose, nothing about them suggested they were interested in buying bread, coffee, or anything else. One flashed his identification.

"INS, sir. We want to have a quick word with you," he said. I took a deep breath. I knew where this was heading.

"OK," I said. "Here I am."

"No," he said gesturing upward with his chin. "Back there." As soon as we stepped into the kitchen, they zeroed in on four of my six workers and carted them off. They were undocumented. I called Jeanie to tell her not to expect me home that night. I had a lot of baking to do.

I fully admit to knowing about their visa issues when I hired these workers. I suppose that the entrepreneur in me understood the yearning for a lucky break, but it was about much more than just giving someone a job. For me, it was about giving hope. As a human being, and immigrant myself, I found it hard to crush someone's dream for a better life, particularly when they're standing before you, eyes pleading for a chance. In each case, I made it clear that their papers had to be sorted out if they were to stay on. INS did in fact clear at least one of the detainees almost immediately. His papers had finally come through just before the raid. In the days that followed, we all rolled up our sleeves at the bakery and grabbed all the extra hands we could. Together we pushed through until I could find new staff.

By this time, I had found a new home for the bakery. Only blocks away, it was an older two-story building covering some fifteen thousand square feet. Its address was a familiar one. East 233rd Street was home to the dairy company I had worked for years before. I wondered whether it was prophetic—and not in a good way. Even then I had to admit that the location was less than ideal. A canal was its immediate neighbor. I worried about rats and other critters.

Then there was its size. I considered the possibility that I was taking on excess square footage. But when I loosely mapped out the equipment we needed, I proved myself wrong. We could easily fill it. Money was my only challenge now. This time I needed a bank loan—and a big one. So I called the Small Business Administration of New York and spoke to a representative. "I need a loan for a bigger place," I said after introducing myself and explaining my position. "I'm being squeezed like toothpaste here."

"How many square feet do you have now?" he asked.

"Two-thousand-five."

"And what are you looking for, sir?"

"There's a place on East 233rd Street by the Hutchinson River—fifteen thousand square feet of almost empty space. It needs work, of course. That's the other reason I need the loan."

I could almost see his eyes widening at the other end of the line. "*Fifteen* thousand? But that's six times more space than you have now."

"That's right."

"Mr. HoSang, it's too big a jump," he replied with a tone that was sincerely apologetic. "I'm really sorry. I wish I could give you the news you want to hear but I just don't think you'll get the loan."

"I know what I need," I said. I was disappointed by his reply, but not offended. It was his job to be cautious. It was mine to push. "I need to be operating under USDA approval. The place we have now is too small to meet their criteria. Our sales are strong and yet we've barely tapped the market. Trust me. We can handle the expansion."

The loan never happened. In hindsight I should have prepared a business plan with an architect's blueprint showing all the equipment I needed, and my current and projected sales. Had I done that, I might have realized that the new location was actually not big enough, and, therefore, dodged the potholes I was about to fall into.

No one knows your business the way you do. The lending institution is there to be persuaded. So persuade them. Present your position in a detailed and professional manner with facts that are indisputable. Show them your performance and your confidence. Then sell them your vision.

I would not know it for a while, but being turned down by the SBA was divine intervention. Still determined to expand and position myself to receive the USDA's blessing, I convinced the tenant at the East 233rd Street location to sublet to us. He was only too happy to oblige.

Now with plans in place to move, I made an appointment to see the Bronx Borough President. Speaking to him by telephone, I explained my plight, and the reason the racks had to sit on the sidewalk a few minutes each morning. I let him see that my actions were not driven by defiance, and showed him that I was already remedying the situation by moving to a new place.

He listened without interrupting me, which gave me hope. When I was finished, he asked me a few more questions, including how much time I needed. I told him four months, one more than I actually needed. To my great relief, he went to bat for me. He promptly called the sanitation department and asked them to give me some wiggle room until I moved into the new facility.

I was breathing again, but my woes had only just begun.

At this point, with just a couple months to go before moving into our new plant, I decided to take a chance and start wholesaling the patties more aggressively. I admit that it was a huge risk, but my adrenaline was pumping too hard. I couldn't sit and wait. It wasn't something I was terribly proud of.

In order to carry out the deed, I turned to some abandoned banana boxes that had been left behind by the bakery's previous owner. It wasn't terribly professional looking, but I couldn't afford to buy real trays. The only tray I had was one left by the Arnold Bread deliveryman after dropping off our order of rolls. So I put it to good use. One day, an Arnold Bread deliveryman happened to be in the same store in which I was making my own delivery, using none other than my "loaner" Arnold Bread tray. After stocking the shelf, I put the tray on the floor and turned to check on another aisle. By the time

I returned, I saw the guy reaching for what he thought was his tray—which it technically was. I lost a perfectly fine tray that day.

Meanwhile, I began work on the second floor of our new place. As I was only doing the bare minimum in the way of renovations, I went into my own pocket to fund the expenses. For equipment, I scoured the *New York Times* and a baker's trade magazine. Between the two, I found used equipment from two bakeries that had gone belly up. The equipment had lost their shine but not their spunk. At any rate, I didn't have a choice. Money was tight. With each piece, we were getting closer to being operational. My wallet wasn't the only thing getting squeezed, however. This time, the USDA inspectors had gotten wind of our most serious infractions. Now we were being written up for illegally wholesaling the patties. I was not in a position to complain. I was breaking the rules and there was no gray area about that.

Frustration nagged at me like a scab that wouldn't heal. The last thing I wanted was to pull the plug on momentum. So, we continued to make the patties at the Dyre Avenue location, transporting them baked to the new location, and storing them there in our brand new walk-in freezer. At first we used a small panel van bearing our logo to move them. But when it was clear that there were eyes on us, I rented a U-Haul truck every now and then to throw off our scent. It worked, but only for a while.

One day I arrived at the bakery to hear that the USDA inspector had just appeared at the new location. Not finding me there, he tagged one hundred cases of patties, and promptly left. I knew better than to stay at the bakery on Dyre. Without a word to anyone, I slipped out and went to the deli next door while keeping a close eye on the street.

Sure enough, the inspector pulled up in his marked vehicle minutes later. I did the only thing that came to mind. I used the deli's phone to call the bakery and asked to speak with Lynn. When he finally came to the phone, I spoke quickly. "Don't say a word, Lynn, it's me. I'm calling from next door."

"O-K…?" he replied.

"The inspector's there, right?"

"Ah…yes. Yes, sir," he said, trying to sound more normal.

"And I guess he's looking for me."

"Correct."

"OK," I said. "Let me think for a second here…Lynn, tell him that I've left for the day running errands, but that I'll be in tomorrow. Got that?"

"Yes." I stayed on the line as my friend covered for me and relayed the message. Less than a minute later he returned.

"Vin, he's gone."

"And…?"

"He said, 'Tell your Mr. HoSang that he had better be here in the morning at nine o'clock sharp, and not a minute later!' Sounds like he means business. What the heck are you going to do?" I squeezed my eyes shut for a few seconds while a thousand thoughts raced in my head.

"I dunno. I have between now and tomorrow to figure it out."

That night I locked my eyes on the ceiling. There wasn't going to be any sleep for me. I had bought myself a few hours to hatch an escape plan, but could think of nothing. Really, there was nothing *to* do. I had been caught, and that was that. I said a prayer for a light punishment—a fine or reprimand, anything but the whole book. I had come too far, and yet I was only just getting started. I just wanted a chance.

I went in the next morning at my usual seven o'clock, the bags under my eyes more pronounced than usual. At nine o'clock on the nose, the shop's front door swung open. A man, looking like he was on a mission, walked in. I took a deep breath. "Mr. HoSang?" he asked. I barely finished nodding in acknowledgment when he began wielding his voice like a machete. He put a hand up as he continued. "No. I don't want to hear anything. Not a single syllable out of you."

I nodded again and held my breath. For a split second I was a kid once more standing before an irate Uncle Harrison. Seconds later, the inspector's voice brought me back to where I now stood—in my own place of business. I straightened up and faced the gentleman squarely while he continued. Sometimes you just have to take what's coming to you. The man continued.

"I know you're wholesaling these patties, so there's no use try-ing to deny it. *But*," he said, only slightly relaxing his tone, "I *am* willing to admit that I have an appreciation for the situa-tion you're in. You're a hard working businessman trying to make a living. From what I've seen, that much is clear."

As the words came out, I wondered if I had held my breath so hard that I was lightheaded and now hearing things. He wasn't finished, though. "So this is what I'm going to do for you. I'm going to have you bring back those tagged boxes at your other location to this location so you can sell them to your retail customers—*directly*. Got me? Retail only. I won't confiscate the patties, even though I could." As he neared the end of his lecture, he seemed to put the machete away. Almost. "Your product is good—I know that. I also know your back is against the wall. Understand that I have no choice but to respond to the calls I get. That's my job, and that's why I'm here today. So, let me be very clear. From here on, don't let me catch you wholesaling again. Now, you have a nice day, sir." With that, he turned and walked out.

It was around then that I had another important visi-tor. This one did not come to reprimand me, however, but to shower me with praises. It was my father.

At ninety-eight, Henry HoSang could barely see through his cataracts, but you wouldn't know it as he shuffled through the bakery while I gave him the tour. All he could do was beam, his eyes shining, as he patted me on the shoulder repeatedly, saying, "You good son. You good son."

That was my father's last visit to New York. To this day, I regret with every fiber of my being that my parents never lived to see the full extent of my achievements, but comfort myself knowing that they lived long enough to see the foundation. Henry HoSang, the gentle father who had been forced to give his children away like a litter of kittens, would draw his last breath a few years later. He was one hundred and three.

. . . .
. . .

CHAPTER 13

. . .
. . . .

The mountain that almost killed me

"Fire in the belly; it's the tonic for success. Without it, you'll struggle when challenges drain you. Your fuel can be anything: the wish to make your parents proud; the desire to live comfortably; the need to be known as an expert at something. Whatever your drive may be, treasure it."

Vincent

WE WERE NEAR THE END OF 1983. THE CLOUDS HAD parted just enough to let a little sunshine through. I had managed to keep at bay potentially sticky situations with two entities: the Department of Sanitation, which had agreed to give us a wide berth, and the United States Department of Agriculture, which had called a conditional truce, thanks to an inspector who was as merciful as he was professional. Matter of fact, the USDA had already approved us for wholesaling, in principle. Once we were fully operational at East 233rd Street, they would then conduct a final inspection and make it official. We were one signature away from that almighty stamp. I could almost smell the ink on the paper. By this time, we'd been operating Royal Caribbean Bakery on Dyre Avenue for almost four years.

Renovation work at the new location was almost finished. In fact, we were already baking our breads and buns on the second floor. All we had left to complete was the bottom floor, where we would produce our patties. Until then, the baking of those pies continued at Dyre.

I confess that I decided to take the USDA inspector's words literally—I would not let him catch me wholesaling. I rolled the dice and took one last chance at "creative sales and marketing," and continued to wholesale. I fully admit that I was taking an incredibly huge risk. This was nothing at all like writing my detention lines in huge letters so I could get out of punishment faster. I don't know what the inspector would have done had he caught me after that spirited, yet extremely generous, warning. I doubt he'd have been as patient a second time around.

Even today, as a man well into his seventies, I think back to that time of my life and try to peek into my younger mind. I would not do today what I did then, but it's easy for me to feel this way now that I've pulled myself out of poverty. Thirty years ago, the yearning to put a significant distance between my childhood and me was strong—almost primal.

Even though I don't regret the path that led me here, it doesn't change the fact that my childhood poverty still defines me. To this day, when I pull up to the gas station and ask the attendant to fill 'er up with high test, I hear myself saying the words as if I were a bystander. The young man in me, the one who often drove his van on fumes, still finds it incredible that he can now take it all the way to the top. The simple luxury of a full tank of gas is something I don't—and never will—take for granted.

I grabbed one more chance to wholesale. All I could see was the finish line, now coming into full view. Not wasting a moment to blink, I pushed even harder to complete what was left of the renovations. God, however, had other plans. When we were less than a month away from completion, the Department of Sanitation returned. This time, they weren't writing about a new violation. This time, they were writing about *their* new plans for *our* property.

I don't know how I didn't collapse to the floor the day I got the letter. Citing *eminent domain*, it explained the Department's intention to convert the building into a sanitation garage. I did the only thing I could think of—I called my attorney and asked him how we could fight our way out of this.

The following morning when I got down on my knees to pray, I closed my eyes and asked God *why*. I didn't understand, I told Him. I had worked hard. I may not have been a total boy scout, but neither was I a ruthless cheat. I wasn't stepping on anyone's toes. I wasn't, as Jamaicans like to say, "boxing the food out of other people's mouths." Looking back, I see now that He wasn't saying, "No, Vincent." He was saying, "Not yet, Vincent, not this."

Our day in court came. Not surprisingly, we lost our appeal. Not only did we lose our lease, we lost all ground we had covered with the USDA. For our inconvenience, the court awarded us relocation compensation. I wasted not even a minute venting. I could not change the court's ruling, but I could change the events that followed. I immediately went in search of a replacement property. It was now 1984.

A few months later, following a relentless search, my realtor called about a factory in nearby Mount Vernon. Owned by three partners, the factory had once been in full swing before losing its sole contract with the military. With no other vendors to absorb the loss, the partners decided to shut down their machines and go their separate ways. The plant was twenty thousand square feet, five thousand more than the property I had just lost, but in much better shape. *I'm gonna get it,* I told myself. When I learned of the asking price, the breath flew out of my lungs—they wanted an even million.

The barefoot Springfield boy in me almost burst out laughing in hysteria. I, Vincent HoSang, a man who once had to budget to buy his weekly newspaper, was now contemplating buying a million-dollar property.

The challenge was that I didn't have the full million. Six hundred thousand dollars was the most the bank was willing to risk on me. What I really needed was $1.2 million so I could buy the place and equip it to my liking. By this time, I had built a strong rapport with the bank. I had met every payment on time and in full, but even a good track record can only stretch so far. And they were not, as they explained, in the real estate business. I would have to find the rest on my own.

So, I did for this property what I did for the bakery. I went to the sellers for a second mortgage. I can't say I went to them brimming with confidence. Four hundred thousand was no chump change. If my own bank, with which I had a solid relationship, did not find it prudent to extend to me the full amount, why would three complete strangers take that chance on an island immigrant with a funny accent?

By now, however, I had learned that America was the land of grit, so I decided to just ask. The worst they could say was no. I told them what I knew for sure—that my business was strong, and that our sales were going through the roof. I looked them in the eye and assured them that I had no plans for failure. After a brief discussion among themselves, they agreed to give me a shot in the wake of their grand adventure's abrupt end. For the second time, I was buying property with little down. As soon as all the requisite paperwork was dotted, crossed and signed, we began working in earnest. Our proposed move-in date was for mid-1986. So began the climb that was Mount Vernon.

Sometimes, inexperience combines with luck to produce a happy result. When David Cybul drew up the blueprints for Mount Vernon, they revealed, much to our surprise, that space was already an issue. If we installed all the machines needed, there'd be no room for the flour. We answered the challenge by putting a silo in the yard, which enabled us to store a trailer and a quarter of flour. Pleased that we cleared the first obstacle, we pressed on past the foothills.

I soon decided that I needed more help, and asked David for the names of general contractors or project managers. He produced the name and number of a young project manager he'd recently met. He'd made an impression of competence, David said, but suggested I keep a close eye on him, as I should do for anyone else. It was, of course, good business advice. I thanked him for his honesty and called the fellow to arrange a meeting.

Just a few years out of college, Bob was a lanky fellow with a stride as easy as his mannerism. I ran him through a rigorous interview, and found him to be both eager and knowledgeable. Finding no obvious objections to speak of, I hired him and hammered out a $60,000 contract. The agreement was that I would cut him a check for $10,000 weekly, and withhold final payment until after I got my certificate of occupancy. The latter provision was, of course, just good business practice.

Renovations began almost immediately. I hovered close, asking all the questions any business owner with two massive loans and a ticking clock would. Renovating was no easy task. As it was, I was being pulled from all directions while trying to get Mount Vernon ready for production. There was new equipment to be purchased and installed, staff to be hired and trained, and the USDA's approval to be secured. So when my project manager assured me that he had his part under control, I was beyond relieved. I could focus on the other hundred pressing matters.

Now relaxed, I turned my attention to the new engineer I had brought in to buy and install the new equipment. With Rick, I signed a contract worth $1.2 million. His job was to source and install the new equipment we needed for the bread line. By our estimates, bread production would not begin for another few months. Fortunately, we were in better shape where our patty production was concerned, as we already had most of the equipment needed. That was one product for which we could not risk any down time. The transition had to be seamless.

Meanwhile, a week or two into the renovation, my initial impression of my project manager had evolved into a comfortably positive one. In fact, I found him to be a generally affable guy who was always ready to talk at length about the job at hand. I thought back to my architect's veiled warning, and decided that David was probably just being overly cautious. Convinced that Bob was "good people," I brought him a bit closer to my inner circle, even inviting him to lunch when time allowed.

With the project's end in sight, I decided one day that, as it was all going smoothly, I would not hold back the last payment. At that point it just felt almost rude to me. Three weeks before the estimated completion date, I handed over the check. With that decision, I removed my previously constructed protective shield and replaced it with a mantle of trust.

The following Monday, Bob arrived at the plant looking a little agitated. Naturally, I asked him what was wrong. He rubbed the back of his head then explained that he was about to have transportation trouble. His car lease was up that Friday. Instead of taking on another lease, however, he was hoping to buy something more modest. The problem was a lack of funds. Would I, he asked, be willing to help him with a small personal loan to make up the balance? As soon as he put the question out there, he immediately assured me that the transaction would be properly documented.

No alarms went off in my head. Even looking back, I still hear none. All I saw was a young man trying to make the right decisions, so I said the words he wanted to hear. "That's not a problem, Bob, I can help out. How much were you thinking of?"

I wrote him a check for $15,000. We drew up a standard demand note to tidy up the transaction, signed it, and sealed it with a handshake. As we clasped hands, the thought flashed in my mind that I might turn the loan into a thank-you gift for a job done well, but I said nothing at the time. I decided to surprise him at the end of the project. Little did I know that the surprise was going to be all mine.

I am, by nature, a handshake kind of man. It's in my DNA to trust. However, I'll be the first to admit that it's a risky way to operate.

Trust in business can either stoke an association into the best of friendships, or burn it to ashes. I've had to learn how to temper that natural inclination to take people at their word. Now I force myself to assess the person before me. I try to anticipate the tricks he or she might be scheming, or the potential strings attached to favors being offered. It's hard to think this way when it goes against your nature. Fortunately, I'm more seasoned now at reading people and their intentions. For me, it's a bit like shaking hands. It doesn't come naturally, but I manage a firm grip with my right hand, even though I'm actually left-handed.

That Friday morning, Bob pulled into the parking lot in his new Ford sedan. Later, as the day drew to a close, he came up to me and asked if I had his check ready. I looked at him as if he had just spoken in a foreign tongue. "Check? What check?" He shoved his hands in his pocket, tilted his chin up, and repeated his request. I blinked and opened my eyes at him. "Bob, I've already paid you in full," I said, unsure if I was misunderstanding him, or just slow to catch an obvious joke. If he was joking he was being quite poker-faced about it. I pressed him again.

"You have the $60,000 we agreed on—paid in full as of last week. Remember?"

This time it was Bob's ear that was malfunctioning. All he did at that point was shrug, rock back on his heels, and advise me that if there were no checks, there'd be no more work. With that he got into the car I had just paid for, and sped off.

I squeezed my eyes shut and shook my head. I had let my guard down, allowed myself to be duped again. Inside, I felt a wince I had not felt in a long time, like a muscle reminding me of an old injury. It wasn't that I was in shock. Desperation could make people do some crazy things. I knew that. This time, it was about ego. Watching Bob drive off in his "grand prize" was downright painful.

Wasting time wallowing in pity is something I never tolerated. I used this personal peeve as an antidote to my sour mood. I needed to move on. I accepted the car incident for what it was—a good reminder to check that blind spot of mine more than once. *Get over it, Vincent,* I told myself. *No one's hurt and you have work to do.* I put it behind me.

We had two weeks of work left and not a second to spare for licking wounds. I jumped up to complete the renovations on my own, which involved some on-the-job learning. Despite Bob's sudden departure, we were able to get our certificate of occupancy in our hands, and on schedule.

Meanwhile, Jeanie and I deliberated like expectant parents on what to call our new company. I felt strongly that our name needed to communicate with our customers. We needed something that told the public where we were from, what we were about, and what kind of experience they would have with our products.

In the end, we decided on Caribbean Food Delights.

CHAPTER 14

Risk—sometimes sweet, sometimes sour

"You'll make mistakes, take wrong turns, and even fall victim to trickery. Successful entrepreneurs—even the most seasoned—will trip and fall; but they always get back on their feet."

Vincent

WE HAD MANAGED TO COMPLETE THE RENOVA-
tion in spite of the cloud of dust generated by the project manager's sudden departure. With our certificate of occupancy now in hand, we cut the proverbial ribbon and hit the start button at the Mount Vernon plant. Once again, I had two huge

concerns on my plate. This time, however, the debt portion was the biggest I'd ever had to swallow. Between the bank and the sellers, I was a little over $4 million in debt. It was 1986, and I was now in my mid-forties. For the first time, I began to sense a slight shakiness in my constitution.

As if qualifying for our USDA approval wasn't stressful enough, the new oven I had purchased for the breads and buns was acting like an untamed animal. For some reason, whatever we produced was coming out either raw or burned. My stomach churned as the pile in the dumpster began to grow. Desperate to end the waste, I called the engineer who had dealt with the oven, and asked him to sort us out. This he did promptly.

For extra support on all things bread and bun, I also reached out to an old friend in Miami who had decades of experience as a master baker with monster machines. Freddie Hugh had once owned a large bakery in Jamaica by the name of Yummy Bakery. Not long after he got my call, Freddie dropped what he was doing in his own business to fly to New York and don the hat of consultant.

My shoulders relaxed at the sight of Freddie in my factory. After giving him the tour, I gave him space so he could make his assessment. At first his instructions seemed counterintuitive. My head baker frowned and tried to argue. But Freddie was quietly confident. Sure enough, a test run yielded the results we wanted. He nodded with satisfaction. "If, after

I leave New York, you're not happy with the results," he said, "call me."

The only call made to him was from me, thanking him once again for his invaluable support. He had helped us over our hurdle. Freddie was one part of our recuperation strategy. I also secured support on the business side by hiring a consultant. Now that we had graduated to another level, I thought it would be wise to get some guidance from another expert.

Meanwhile, with the bread oven now in full swing, we turned our attention to our USDA status for the Jamaican patties. The goal post for my USDA approval had moved, but I was not disheartened. I felt instinctively happier with the Mount Vernon plant. Its location alone was far better. It had none of the potential issues that the East 233rd Street property presented. There was no canal behind us, and no second story to complicate workflow and logistics. I was confident that once we got all our equipment in place, the USDA would bless us once and for all.

By this time, the engineer had installed most of the equipment for our bread production. Already in place were some of the bigger ones like the oven, molder, and proof box. My adrenaline level spiked with each one we installed without any hiccups. I knew then that I must have been an engineer in another life. (My pulse still quickens when a machine performs like a superhero. It's the reason I'm a little addicted to the television shows *How It's Made* and *Food Factory*.)

Thankfully, there had been only one glitch up to this point. One of the smaller pieces (called a *sheeter*) that we'd bought from a Pennsylvania company failed to work properly. When we discovered the issue, our engineer, Rick, jumped on the matter and took care of its immediate return and replacement. Still unsettled from what had gone down with the project manager, I was secretly relieved for Rick's quick action to correct the situation. The last thing I needed was a delay, or complications of any kind. I needed to return to full production mode. I had loans deadlines to meet with no stretch in them.

At first, the debt I had taken on was a pebble in my shoe. Now, it was a growing blister gnawing into my heel. Inside me waged a quiet battle between the best of my intentions and the worst of my fears. I knew what I was capable of. I knew the vision I had carefully nurtured over the years. I knew I could do it, but I couldn't ignore the potential issues developing ahead as I slowly made the steep trek. If the cracks were big enough, I could potentially slip right through them and be swallowed whole. Even though I had a dedicated army behind me, the risk that was mine made this a journey of one.

All I could do now was acknowledge my fears and walk past them. Each morning, as I got down on my knee, I asked God to walk with me for a little while. *Please*, I said, *don't let me trip and fall now. It's a long way down.* Looking back, I can say that while I may have learned about God on the hill in Springfield, I really got to know Him on my mountain.

By this time, our young engineer had almost become a fixture at the plant. At just over six feet with a shock of red hair, he was hard to miss. Now entering the final leg of the project, he had met most of his obligations as outlined in our contract. All that was left to arrive were just a couple pieces. *Almost there*, I told myself. *Almost there.*

One day, sometime in the morning, Rick paid me a surprise visit at my new Mount Vernon office. After giving me his usual friendly greeting blended in with a couple of lighthearted jokes, he made what seemed to be a mundane request. He was wondering whether he could borrow my copy of our contract so he could refresh his memory on one of the details listed. He was on his way to see a new prospect for preliminary contract negotiations, and suddenly remembered one item that he wanted to include.

I admit I found it a tad odd that Rick seemed unprepared for his meeting. From the beginning, he had been quite professional and on the ball. Rubbing his nose as he usually did—the poor guy seemed to suffer from chronic allergies—he offered a detailed explanation about wanting to spin around and return to his office for his copy, but that after assessing the heavy traffic and dwindling time, he figured on stopping by our plant since he was closer. I interrupted him with a smile and wave of my hand. "Sure, Rick. Not a problem," I said, reaching over to my safe where I kept such precious documents. He continued talking as I pulled out the file.

Taking another audible sniff while I dug up the contract, he suggested that, since he was already here, he'd save himself another trip by collecting the balance of the payment for the remaining equipment. "No problem," I said. I rang up our accountant and requested the check. A few minutes later he had both the contract and check in his hands. "Go ahead and use my desk if you'd like," I said, gesturing to the chair beside him. Just at that point, I got a call. As I signaled an apology with my free hand, Rick blurted something about grabbing a quick lunch from out front while I took my call.

That was the last I saw of him. At first I assumed that he'd gone into the plant after his "quick lunch." When I asked around, I learned that Rick had left. When I didn't hear from him for the rest of the day, I assumed that he'd moved on to his appointment. When the next day came and I still had not heard from him, the panic swooped down and grabbed me like an eagle claiming its prey.

Rick had fallen off the radar. I made multiple calls to his office. None made it through. Confusion rolled in like a sandstorm. *This can't be happening*, I told myself. *Not again.* Then the questions started coming at me like missiles. He had just gotten the final check from me for the balance of the equipment. What was going on? Had he taken ill? Was he caught up in another job? Had there been an accident?

A couple days later I drove to his office, which was about two hour's drive away. Stuck to the door was the bankruptcy notice, and another advising of an equipment auction being held not long from then.

Back at my office, I wiped away the cold sweat and called the vendor from whom we were buying one of the last pieces of equipment. That's when the fuzziness cleared to show the real picture—sharp edges and all. "I'm so sorry, Mr. HoSang," the agent said, "but your engineer had only *inquired* about the machine. He didn't actually place an order for one. And as there was no deposit made, we have nothing secured for you. Is it possible that he made arrangements with another company? I'm sure that's what happened."

I put the phone into the receiver and lowered my head into my hands. I let the world around me go dark and silent. My breathing immediately became shallow. My heart pounded so hard I was sure it was going to explode out of my chest. Once again, I had been swindled. I thought back to Rick's initial sterling performance, including his quick action with the malfunctioning sheeter. Was it all part of the plan? A ploy to relax my guard? Had he coaxed me into trusting him over something small so he could move in for something big?

This time I had to fight the urge to react openly. That had never been my way. I wanted neither my family nor my staff to suffer for my mistakes. But this time, panic slammed me like a rogue wave. What I had lost to Bob was a joke compared to the six-figure check I had just handed over to Rick. The money, part of the loan I had taken out, was not mine to lose. Yet, just like that, it was gone.

My life hit pause without warning. Up until then, I had always been the kind of person who woke up each day knowing exactly how I was going to fill it. Now I woke up feeling lost. I started to drink. As alcohol goes, I was in the minor league. The occasional beer was the most I'd have. Now it was my breakfast beverage of choice. Sometimes, I'd have as many as four in a row. No one commented openly, but I saw the double glances and raised eyebrows.

In the nights that followed, I had to will my mind to rest. In the days, the circles under my eyes showed the sleep that had eluded me. Food became something I pushed around on my plate. Socializing, once a pleasure, became a chore I avoided. King was one of the few people I wanted to speak with. He'd been a witness to my entire life. It meant something each time he told me I'd get through this. Even my brother's support could not hold me up for long, however. The days and weeks crawled by. One day, I caught my image in the mirror and saw a confused man with fear in his eyes. It was the closest I had come to not knowing myself. My doctor prescribed some Valium and issued the warning to relax, or brace myself for a heart attack.

I was veering dangerously close to the precipice. The only way to retreat was to focus my attention on the immediate future. It took every ounce of energy I had in me, but I forced myself to focus on what was positive in the present.

After months of producing our first television commercial, we launched our first major marketing campaign, which included English and Spanish channels. Despite the chaos around me, I felt a small ripple of excitement in my veins. We were putting ourselves out there more than ever. The only thing was, we were getting ahead of ourselves and didn't realize it. Our commercials worked beautifully, prompting customers to go looking for our Jamaican patties. But when those customers couldn't find them because we had not adequately supplied the market, they merely gave their business to our competitor. It was another blow we couldn't afford. Now reeling from the crippling one-two punch, I barely had the presence of mind to make a mental note of my mistake: don't advertise ahead of your distribution capability. I vowed that it would never happen again.

Anxious to straighten the wheel of what now felt like a skidding car, I looked for help beyond my immediate circle. At the suggestion of my architect, David, I went to see another peer by the name of Tom Rotinelli. He was a business-friendly Italian American whom I had met through David. I had always liked Tom's no-frills approach, and found him to be consistently genuine. He was just as competitive as the next man, but never cagey. I sat with him one day in his office at his pasta factory in New Rochelle. With no attempt at hiding my anxiety, fatigue painted on my face like a carnival mask, I explained my predicament, and ended with the frank admission that I was in trouble. I needed help.

Tom sat back in his chair, his chin resting on his fingers that were in steeple formation. He listened quietly the entire time I unloaded, nodding every so often. I didn't have to explain how I was feeling. He knew. So it must have taken a lot of courage for him to offer what ended up being one of the best pieces of advice I've ever received. "Vin," he said, leaning forward on his desk. "Let me tell you what I've learned in business. If you can go it alone, do it alone. Try your level best to get through this rough patch. Yeah, it's scary as hell. I know how that feels—knots in your stomach like you swallowed marbles…little or no sleep…you walk around like you're crawling through the desert with no oasis on the horizon. But at least you're still moving *forward*, my friend, even if it's an inch at a time. You'll get there, but if after your best efforts you find you still need a partner, yeah, sure, I'll come in with you."

We chatted a bit longer. Already I felt better for having shared my woes with a fellow entrepreneur, someone who truly understood both sides of the risk we faced, day after grueling day. I thanked him and returned to my own factory, knowing that he had spoken the truth, and that I had just been given good old-fashioned sound advice. I have never forgotten Tom's kindness.

I stayed in the ring, fighting for my livelihood. Along with a couple others from my staff, I continued meeting with the business consultant I had hired. I admit that I was still wrapping my fingers around the necks of beer bottles at this point. In fact, I almost nodded off in the middle of one of our meetings. I caught myself in time to hear him comment that, by the looks of it, Mr. HoSang was going nowhere fast. His assessment, in his defense, was not an unfair one. I was not at my finest.

One morning, after plummeting into a few days of near listlessness, I opened my eyes and drew in a deep breath. As I lay quietly in my bed, I saw images of my childhood flash before me: our tiny hut with the flimsy zinc roof, the tiny shop that barely sustained us, the creditors coming back for their goods. I thought about the moment my father delivered the worst news of our lives. His ordeal had been much worse than mine. I pictured his face, awash with bravery, as he executed his painful plan to send us all away. He had saved us, though. In the end, we survived.

I touched the scar on my arm. My parents had sacrificed much to give us a chance. I needed to honor that. I had worked every day since then to get to this point. Every day. I couldn't give up now. This was not about being rich. This was about the courage to take my rightful place in this world. *Enough*, I said to myself. *Let's get on with it.*

I got up, splashed cold water on my face, and went down on both knees this time. Eyes closed, I asked God to forgive me for surrendering to fear, and turning to alcohol instead of Him. Then I asked for the strength to muscle up once again. I was about to make a decision for which I needed His guidance. I promised that if He could see me through this next step,

I would forever be His faithful servant. I would pass on the blessings a thousand-fold.

From where I stood—almost knee-deep in quicksand—there were only two choices at my disposal. Either I folded, or I asked the bank for another loan. There was no rich uncle to whom I could turn for a safety net. If I *did* have one, he hadn't yet shown his face. I would have to find my own way out of this mess.

The first scenario did not appeal to me. I was not about to hoist the white flag and slink off with my tail between my legs. I was no longer a boy in "short pants" as Jamaicans like to say. I was a man with a family to support. Then there were my workers. Their lives relied on my success, too. They had their own dreams to plant and grow. In my mind, it had to be Plan B, as in *B* for *bank*. I shared my decision with my accountant. He didn't hesitate to give me the thumbs up. "Well," I said, "I guess this is what they mean by sink or swim." It was time to venture into the deep.

A few days later, I found myself before my bank's loan officers. They had come to see us on our turf. Feeling as if I were sitting naked before a panel of judges, I connected the dots for them. I told them that a couple scam artists had relieved me of a couple hundred grand. I therefore needed another loan of $600,000 so I could finish the final leg of the renovation, and secure the balance of the equipment. The renovation work must be completed, I said, so that I could begin production.

And production must begin so that I could start honoring my original loans. As for this new loan on the table, if they agreed to lend it to me, I would commit to repaying it within a year, in full.

I can't remember the exact words I used, but that was the opening of my "presentation" to the panel of stunned eyes and, I'm sure, disbelieving ears. His exact words escape me now, but one gentleman asked, with a small laugh, if I had lost my mind. The bank had lent me all it could. The laugh I remember for sure. But I didn't react. Instead, I took it on the chin. I remember my poor bank manager shifting in his chair and clutching at his tie a couple times. He had warned me ahead of time not to get my hopes up. "Vincent, not only are you already getting our ceiling offer, you're up to your nose in debt. It's not looking good." This meeting, which included his immediate boss, was his last-ditch attempt to get me the loan.

It wasn't easy sitting there, staring at what essentially amounted to strangers, asking them to toss you a lifeline while they analyzed you. It was almost humiliating having to admit that I'd been conned like an amateur. In many ways I suppose that's what I was, new at the game, but I didn't let that throw me off. I had already made peace with the fact that I was meant to be here. This was just another opportunity to prove myself.

For the duration of the meeting I did not entertain the thought of failure. I did the opposite. I pictured myself getting that check, and cutting the ribbon at the grand opening of my new facility, smiles all around me. Soon, my breathing became easy and calm, my speech clear and deliberate. Clasping my hands, I leaned into the table and continued to address my guests. I still can't say what I'd have done had they turned me down, but, in my heart, I know I'd have figured it out—because there is *always* a way.

The laughter did not persist. Once more, the good Lord showed me mercy and kindness. Instead of embarrassing me in my own place of business, the bank's officers looked at my case through the eyes of professionals. While there was insanity in my situation, there was also logic in my thinking. If I sank and declared bankruptcy, their books would take a hit. I had not failed them up to that point. There was no argument there. My numbers were strong. No question about that. Also strong was my determination to succeed. I sat there as they weighed the situation.

That day, the bank's team left with a decision in my favor. The terms, however, were stringent. I had one year in which to repay this new loan, and not a day over. I promised them that their faith in me would not go unrewarded.

Then I promised God and myself that, one day, I would smile at this moment, and maybe even laugh a little, too.

CHAPTER 15

Stamp of approval

"Don't be complacent, even if you're at the top. A new kid on the block will come along and change all that if you're not paying attention. At the time of the writing of this book, we are one of the leading producers of (frozen) Jamaican food products in the world. I can't allow myself to feel giddy over that. I don't—and won't—assume that we'll always hold that title."

Vincent

WE WERE MIDWAY THROUGH 1987. WITH THE extra $600,000 loan from the bank, we were finally able to secure the rest of the equipment and install it. Not surprisingly, our rogue engineer never resurfaced. The stunt he pulled faded to a bad memory. While I still quietly chided myself for being so incredibly naive, I didn't allow the experience to erode my confidence. I kept my head faced forward. Rick seemed like a bright kid with a great future ahead. Why some chose to misappropriate their talent and opportunities was something I'd never understand.

Six months after moving in, we finally received USDA approval. Now free to wholesale our meat patties to our heart's content, we were about to meet our assigned resident inspector. I spent much of that day walking on air like a teen on his first day with his driver's license. Our business had finally grown up. With the chaos finally in the rearview mirror, I swore to myself that I would never expand the factory again. *That's it*, I said to myself. *No more.*

At first I was apprehensive about meeting our inspector. I didn't know what it would be like operating with our own resident "god." But my fears were unfounded. To my relief, we were blessed with one who seemed to operate somewhere between textbook-strict and real-world reasonable. I could live with that. Ironically, however, getting that all-important USDA approval also came with some built-in challenges. Not only did the factory itself have to be in compliance, so did the product. Now we had to use a little more beef and a little less water. We went to work to adjust the formula.

I like formulation. I trust it. If there was one item about which I was (and still am) particularly fussy, it was our patty. We had gone to great lengths to get the taste and texture just right. We had broken down the formula to exact measurements, even taking into account the weight of the container in which the spices came. It was a process to which I was unrelentingly dedicated. So when we made the adjustments to satisfy USDA requirements, and ended up with a patty that may as well have been someone else's, I almost broke out into another round of cold sweat.

I was caught between a rock and a hard place. I needed to produce to generate sales. At the same time, if I didn't produce something worthy of my customers' support, if I didn't give my faithful supporters the taste they had come to love, sales would suffer. That could not happen. Determined to get the taste we wanted, we hammered at it, nonstop, until our new USDA-approved version was almost the original's twin.

The pieces were snapping back into place. We were finally the bosses of our new equipment. Then there was the product itself. Not only had we caught our patty formula once more, production was humming along like a Broadway musical. Now basking under the watchful eye of the USDA, we were pushing the wholesale side of the business as if it were the first time a Jamaican patty had landed on American soil. Meanwhile, our inspector continued to be as thorough in his duty as were we in our drive to comply. It was a match as good as one could get.

It was then that I hired a full-time sales manager. While I had been the one to fill that role when we were still inching along, we were now in a completely different league. Our new sales manager went door to door in search of our big break. Before long, we were shaking hands with the popular supermarket chain A&P (The Great Atlantic and Pacific Tea Company). They agreed to try our product in two hundred of their stores. I was so charged, I didn't sleep for a week. That such a well-known chain thought our products worthy of its shelf space was a stamp of approval of a different kind.

Naturally, the business agreement came with its industry terms and conditions, which included a standard slotting fee. The slotting fee is, for all intents and purposes, a one-time payment to the supermarket for the privilege of occupying its highly sought after shelf space or, as was the case for us, precious freezer space. At that time, A&P's was $10,000 per product. As we had two—mild and spicy beef patties—our check to them was for $20,000. That, of course, was paid whether your products sold or not. I inhaled deeply as I accepted the pain that came with joining in the game. *Consider it a rite of passage,* I told myself. Today, slotting fees, in general, are considerably more. I mention this fee not just to educate aspiring entrepreneurs, but also their would-be employees. It might be helpful to remember that, before he or she was able to hire you, your boss first had to survive an obstacle course riddled with risk.

Our first stab at the mass market did not go as well as we'd hoped. In a way, I believe it was simply not our time. One hiccup was the inability to offer proper tastings. As we were still only wholesaling patties with unbaked crusts, it was cumbersome to arrange for prebaked patties to be taken to the stores for face-to-face demonstrations. In the end, we lost the chance at traction with A&P, but gained experience.

Not long after, one of the major cruise lines expressed keen interest in our cocktail beef patties. Not only did they love the taste, they felt the convenient appetizer size made for ideal bar snacks. My adrenaline rushed. When I took a hard look at the numbers, though, I knew we couldn't handle the volume needed. We had learned from our A&P experience that it's better to admit when you're not ready. And, so, as flattered and excited as we were, we declined to take the plunge. We did, however, take their interest as another confirmation that we had something good in our product.

While sales grew steadily, we sacrificed comfort for profit by operating without some of the frills that would have made life easier—frills like a forklift. We were still taking our meats and beef suet from Oteri's at this point, but his delivery truck did not have a lift gate. Our manager, Selly, came up with the great idea of placing huge old tires beneath the back of the truck so that the boxes could be dropped without breaking open. It worked like a charm. At home, my family made lifestyle sacrifices as well. As a result, we made our loan payments on time. Within a year, we paid off the supplement loan and put a good dent in the others. The couple years that followed brought us increased sales. I couldn't stop smiling inside, and even began to wonder if Mount Vernon would be a repeat of Dyre Avenue. I wondered if we would have to consider expansion shortly after moving in. We had caught a nice rhythm again.

Or so I thought.

At this point, with my children growing and our profits building, I decided that I would soon turn my attention to finding us more living space. Jeanie had long been patient and understanding about our cramped abode while I worked to whittle down our debt, build our business, and increase our cash reserves for the future. I promised myself that a nicer home was the next big project. I wanted nothing more than to provide for my family and make them happy.

By now we had operated out of the Mount Vernon plant for three or four years. Caribbean Food Delights was on its way to becoming the success I had hoped for. Just as I was feeling truly settled in, however, I suffered a rude awakening.

One morning, I was "advised" that my staff had decided to unionize. I won't deny that I took it as a slap in the face. I had been more than generous, not only with their wages, but with my consideration to their personal situations. I had reached into my own pocket many times over. In fact, I had even sponsored a couple workers so that they could get their papers in order.

Bewildered, I took their move in silence. I sat at the negotiating table, nodding as the representative put forth their demands. I agreed to every single one. I was *that* taken aback.

In hindsight, I should have secured myself proper counsel, and counter negotiated.

When it comes to unions, I am of two minds. I know that its main purpose is to ensure fair treatment. To that extent I agree with, and understand, the need for unions. Without a doubt, there are employers who take advantage of their workers. That said, there is another side to it. A union is a lot like a business. It collects fees and has a membership body to which it is accountable. Its mission is to satisfy its members. Therefore, if you're a union member paying fees year after year, it stands to reason that you're going to expect more and more.

I admit that I felt hurt by my workers' decision. I knew in my heart that I had already shown myself to be a good leader—a loyal and protective one. *Yes* I expected the work to be done, no question about that. Every employer does. But I was nothing if not fair and considerate—all of my workers were paid above minimum wage. I had other long-term plans for benefits that would give them even more peace of mind. But I was not yet in a position to do so. I needed more time. I was not raised on a diet of instant gratification. I knew the merit of patience, and that even better days were ahead. I can only assume that our workers were unwilling to wait, or felt unsure of my intentions. I'll never know. In the end I did not allow their sting to fester. I looked past it. With the union in place, we all returned to work.

Then, one day, I got a call from someone identifying him-self as Inspector Police. But all I heard was *police*. I grimaced and jumped to conclusions.

"Police? Oh, my God! Charles…!" I shouted, trying to get his attention. "Charles what have you done now?"

My initial and terribly unfair reaction was based on the fact that our dear Charles had been known to bend a few traffic laws every now and then. But it turned out that this was not a police inspector as thought, but a new USDA inspector whose last name was Police. The inspector was making a preliminary call before taking over the duties of our outgoing inspector. As Charles was our production manager, he was the contact. I breathed a sigh of relief. But I did so too soon.

From the second he stepped through our doors, I knew that this inspector would be different. There was something about the way his eyes penetrated whatever fell in their range of sight—including us. I ignored the unsettled feeling. *Everyone's different*, I reasoned quietly. Instead, I told myself that we would simply operate as we did under the original inspector. Surely the standards would be the same.

This time, my instincts were right. We had begun a new chapter. Before, we barely gave our inspector reason to call our attention to oversights, mistakes, or improper procedures. Now, we could do no right.

At first the new inspector called out small, almost insig-nificant issues. We questioned nothing and addressed each one. On occasion, he'd come up with a more legitimate complaint. One such example was the case of the "roving raisins." The workers in the bread and bun section were tracking raisins into the patty section with their shoes. The reason for that slip was simple. Even though a wall separated the two areas, the workers shared a common locker room. We addressed the concern to his satisfaction. But where a few of his complaints were reasonable, I felt that most were questionable.

I did not have an issue with authority. My goal was to have a first-class operation. If this inspector's vigilance meant a better product for us, then we were on the same side. He was, after all, just doing his job, and I respected that. I did not, however, like the disruption to our workflow. If I didn't know better, I'd have thought that he was enjoying wielding his power more than anything else.

For a while I held my tongue. I prayed that our immediate efforts to achieve compliance would give him reason to relax. I was wrong. Instead, the situation only worsened.

One day, he issued a complaint about the parking lot. As was our custom, we swept the yard once the trucks left to make their deliveries. One day, our inspector decided otherwise. He closed the gate, wrote us up, and had us clean the yard while the trucks were still in the lot. Asking him to allow our delivery trucks to head out first only seemed to harden his resolve. He refused to let a single vehicle in or out until we had swept and washed down the entire place. Needless to say, our deliveries were hours late that day. Our customers were understanding, but not amused. As a result of our delay, they had to face their own unhappy customers.

Heated blow-ups between the inspector and our manager erupted intermittently from this point on. A perpetual frown replaced the smile I used to wear on my commute to work. My morning prayers were more focused. Instead of asking for guidance in general, I directed my pleas to the current thorn in my side. *Please, God*, I'd pray. *Help me to survive this new inspector.*

As if God was trying to confirm my suspicions, the inspector threw another challenge at us after the parking lot incident. While making his usual morning rounds, he came across a light fraying at the edge of one of the canvas conveyor belts in the patty line. Naturally, he brought it to my attention. Naturally, I remedied the issue. I trimmed the belt as instructed, washed the whole system down, then waited for him to give us the green light so we could resume production.

And so we waited.

And waited.

When we reminded him that the belt was ready for inspection, he said he'd be there "shortly." By the time he finally showed up, hours had passed. I looked at my watch. It hardly made sense to start production at that point. Shaking my head, I sent the workers home. I had lost an entire day. Perhaps that single day of lost time seemed insignificant to him. It is entirely possible that he genuinely saw the lost shift as just a drop in the pond. I saw it differently. For anyone who's ever had to ensure that there's money at the end of the week to make payroll, to pay bills, and to protect your investment, each minute wasted, lost, or mismanaged, hurts.

I was furious. It had been a long time since I felt that kind of anger. In an unfiltered moment, I told him outright that I felt he had gone too far. I did not yell, use obscenities, or even go red in the face. I just said the words while looking him squarely in the eye.

I left the plant that day in a fog of disbelief. All the way home I thought about what had happened. It was one thing for someone to do his or her job. It was quite another to take it to what felt like the extreme. I wondered if God was testing me.

The good thing about fogs is that they eventually clear up. After simmering quietly for several days, a light flickered in my head. USDA inspectors were assigned to territories. If I could find a location outside of Mount Vernon, I could bid him farewell. If I could find a bigger place that allowed me to focus on the patties, then we could really take our product into the stratosphere.

For a while, I sat with the idea. I told myself it would be like starting over again…an incredible move…at a whole new level. I thought back to the struggle I had endured just to get here. *Vincent, are you sure about this?*

That day, I must have been in the mood for an extra serving of risk, with a little spice on top. I grabbed the phone and dialed my realtor's number.

"Bill," I said, "Vincent HoSang here. How are you? Good…Yes, we're fine, thank you…Bill, listen, I need you to find me another plant outside of this area…Yes, you heard me right. I'm ready to take this operation elsewhere…Yes…I couldn't be more sure."

CHAPTER 16

Gearing up for more

"While it is true that money can't buy you happiness, financial security is to your life what vitamins are to your body; it boosts your general well-being."

Vincent

IT WAS NOW 1989. AFTER SURVIVING A COUPLE hairpin bends with cash flow and a harrowing ride with our USDA inspector, Caribbean Food Delights was operating once more at a steady pace at its new Mount Vernon plant.

I had emerged from the experience somewhat shaken, but still in the race. If anything, it raised my threshold for tolerance and perseverance. The reinforcement came at the right time. My repeated prayers to the good Lord for a new inspector had gone unanswered. This one, it seemed, was here to stay. I decided to keep my complaints under lock and key while I hatched an escape plan. If I couldn't change the inspector, I would change whom he inspected—it would no longer be us. We were going to move our entire patty production out of Mount Vernon. The decision to relocate would prove to be a pivotal moment for us.

Once again, God was forcing my hand. I could not have known it then, of course, but our ever-vigilant inspector would turn out to be yet another blessing in disguise. Now, when something seemingly negative happens, I always look to see what positive opportunity or lesson it holds. And, in fact, something wonderful did come out of that unhappy situation.

With one eye on plans for increased production, I kept another on new wholesaling opportunities. Day after day my mind churned while our hands, muscles, and machines kept producing those patties. Sometimes, when taking one of my many walks through the plant, I'd think back to some of the hurdles we had cleared. I remembered every bead of sweat that had brought us this far—and every hour spent making the wheels turn. The boy from Springfield was making something of his life. The image of the leap I had taken kept me smiling, even when fatigue and frustration had me by the throat.

Sometime early that year, I received a surprise call from an acquaintance. It was Aston Lue, the New York Life Insurance agent who had passed by some eight years before while I was on the ladder at Dyre Avenue. Since that first meeting, he, too, had been busy making something of his life. He had switched gears, in fact, retiring his insurance salesman hat for that of food distributor. His Miami-based company was just a couple years old. He had not forgotten us, he said, nor had he forgotten our delicious patties. Now he wanted to distribute them in South Florida. His request confirmed in my mind that Caribbean Food Delights had found fertile soil in the United States.

Our business relationship took off with a seamless start. When he called me a few months later out of the blue, I was happy to hear from him. This time, the call had nothing to do with business—he needed a helping hand:

> "I returned to the New York tristate area in 1989 to attend my college class's fifteen-year reunion in Connecticut. By then I had only just started doing business as a young entrepreneur with Vinnie. Still swamped in the foundation years of wearing multiple hats—salesman, deliveryman, receptionist, customer serviceman, and marketing manager—I had uncharacteristically slipped in my duties as administrator, and allowed my paperwork to suffer. Among the casualties was my American Express credit card bill. Being the owner of a start-up company, it was my only credit card at the time.

"Unfortunately, I only came to be aware of the problem while standing at the rental car agency at the JFK International Airport. The only other option, said the representative as she returned the declined card, was to put down $300 in cash. As it turned out, that was pretty much all the money I had on me. I ran through the names of anyone I knew in the area. That's when Vincent's name popped into my head. I borrowed the agency's phone and smiled the second he answered. After explaining my predicament, he replied with a reassuring, 'Sure, let's see what we can do. Stay put. I'll come pick you up.' And so, in true Vinnie style, he dropped what he was doing to help a fellow.

"When he arrived, we greeted one another with a firm handshake and easy conversation. It had been some eight years since we'd spoken in person, and I could see that Vinnie had gone through his share of sleepless nights. While his physical appearance had worn a little, his spirit of kindness was stronger than ever. On arrival at the plant, he pressed the keys to his jeep in the palm of my hand. 'Enjoy your reunion,' he said. 'The tank is full.' This was only our second face-to-face conversation. The vehicle he was lending me was just as new. It had only 2,600 miles on the odometer. Before returning the vehicle to Vinnie, I had it professionally detailed and buffed to a showroom shine.

"From that moment on, I began to see Vinnie not just as a successful businessman, but as a super human being—and personal role model. We had only just become business associates a few months prior to this. We weren't strangers, nor were we close friends. Yet he had not hesitated to bail me out of a situation without hesitation, even though I'm sure he was quite inconvenienced. Today, I am a little older and have met many individuals through business. I can't say I've met many who trust with such an open heart.

"The rest, as they say, is history. Today, Vinnie and I are good friends and associates. The close connection has given me a front row view of his performance over time, and under different circumstances. I've watched him remain even-keeled while under pressure. I've seen him transfer his foundation of integrity to his products. And I've witnessed him grow a business that most can only dream of. "Now in his seventies, he is still leveraging to improve, still keeping a sharp eye on efficiency and technology, still reaching for progress. Entrepreneurs could take a cue from that. Vincent understands that the one with the most risk on the line does not have the luxury of pulling back. The competition won't let you rest. What I admire most is that while he's still at the top of his game, he is incredibly low-key. He may not wear a Rolex, but he has a Rolex operation. It is so pristine, it's almost sterile.

"I recall visiting him at his Tappan plant once. It was a Saturday, and I was marveling at his incredible operation. 'Vinnie,' I said, 'you're at the pinnacle of success. Why are you still here on weekends? Why are you still pushing so hard?' He paused for a few seconds, giving that shy smile I saw at our first meeting. In fact, save for a few gray hairs, a few more pounds around the middle, and some soft wrinkles, he looks today as he did then: seventies haircut, cotton slacks slightly frayed at the ends, basic shirt, and comfortable loafers. 'Aston,' he said, 'I've been poor before. I don't ever want to be poor again.'

"Today, he is rich in many ways. The remarkable thing is that Vinnie employed what textbooks teach without having had the benefit of said books. Instead of complaining, instead of making excuses, he leveraged what he had: wisdom, common sense, drive, and perseverance. With those qualities, he built a good mousetrap. What makes him an anomaly is that he is trusting to the point of being vulnerable, and that he trampled on no heads to get to his destination. Now *that* makes him a true success."

Aston Lue
Fellow Entrepreneur

Our search for a new home continued. That year, I came across an ad in the *New York Times* for a new housing development in a town called Pleasantville. I liked the name, so we took a drive out there to see how it looked and felt. We loved it immediately. Nestled amid tall, elegant pine trees and perched on a low-rising slope, the small neighborhood community was a far cry from the small three-family nest we had in the more densely packed Bronx. At the time, only a few houses had been built in the quiet, picturesque cul-de-sac, but it was enough for us to see what the future neighborhood would look like. *We could be coming home to this every day*, I said to myself.

Pleasantville was everything we'd been clamoring for—space and comfort. Space inside and out was more than generous. After going over the builder's plans, we chose our favorite design, made a few minor changes, and signed on the dotted line. Still bound to a few loans, I was forced to take out a large mortgage. I would have preferred to put down more of a deposit, but my pockets were bordering on empty. Nevertheless, I went with my gut feeling and bought the house. We weren't just moving. We were finally moving up.

It is a widely accepted business tenet that one should use other people's money (such as the bank's) to invest in your business. I agree with this, but only to an extent. While loans enable you to take advantage of an opportunity, it is better to pay off your debt sooner rather than later. This means staying on top of your interest payments and knocking down that principal as soon as you can. If you let interest accrue, you're essentially paying a higher rate on money you've "given" to the bank.

It was in our beautiful Pleasantville home that our children completed their growing years:

"Moving to Pleasantville meant more than just moving into a bigger house where we each had our own room. For me it was like moving to a new country.

"Life in the Bronx had been so different. Those were the early years when our parents worked nonstop at their start-up, seven days a week. It wasn't just any business—it was bakery life. For a while, Dad was someone I only got a glimpse of now and then. I'd get up in the mornings for school, long after he'd left. Mom took care of breakfast and the school runs. I'd only see Dad at night if I stayed up for help with math homework, which he always gave patiently no matter how exhausted. He did make the effort for a few family vacations, though, including an eleven-day trip to Europe, and the occasional jaunt to Disney World or to the Rye Playland theme park in New York. But since most of my friends in the Bronx had similar situations—parents with inflexible work schedules—it all felt normal. That's why, even though it was only thirty minutes away, Pleasantville was culture shock.

"Suddenly I was mixing with kids whose parents were so involved in their lives, about the only thing they didn't do was take over the classroom. They were at every school event, especially if it involved sports. I grew up knowing so little about sports, it was practically a foreign language. It just didn't figure much in our family. Then along came an invitation to join the high school's foot-ball team. I told them I didn't have the experi-ence, but they told me I had the height and build for the game. I joined in my senior year.

"The real shock came the day of my first game. While making my way back to the locker room when it was over, I suddenly heard what sounded like my name above the noise. It was a familiar voice so I stopped, spun around, and scanned the crowd. That's when I caught the arms of someone waving wildly as if putting out a fire. It was Dad. It was like seeing an alien in plain view. I smiled behind the cover of my helmet. That football stadium was the last place I expected to see him, not so much because it was a sports event, but because it was a Saturday, his busiest day.

"He didn't attend too many games after that, but made time for other important moments, like the prom. I wanted to skip it, but Dad wouldn't have it. I found that strange, given that he had not had a prom, but I suppose that that was the reason behind his insistence. Not only did he take me tuxedo hunting, he bought me the tuxedo instead of renting it. He did the same when it came to suits. It was important to always have at least one good one ready, he'd say. So, the man who had neither the time nor patience for malls took me shopping. I still remember looking at him while he was sifting through the racks, and wishing that the day would crawl by so I'd have more time with him.

"Teaching us to drive was another task he took on. He didn't send us to driving school. No, he got into that car with us. Of course, when we were finally getting our cars, Dad never failed to tell us how lucky we were to have such luxuries. Naturally, we had to hear about his feet being his mode of transportation at seventeen, or a lucky ride aboard the back of a dirty delivery truck.

"Dad was always in teaching mode, though. When he could, he'd tell us stories about how poverty made him creative. Like when it was time for us to get our geometry sets. Suddenly, he's showing us how to use any straight-edged object to draw a line, or how to draw a perfect circle using a string, a pencil, and a fixed object. He tried to share glimpses of his earlier poverty on visits to Jamaica as young kids, but we were too young to appreciate it.

"I learned more about Dad once I graduated from college and started traveling with him for business. Usually the trips took us to Las Vegas or larger cities where gambling was sometimes available. I loved Vegas because of the action and energy, but Dad never gambled. Buying lottery tickets was as far as he'd go.

"Years later, I discovered blackjack. I bought books, studied the game, and began playing for fun. One Sunday, I managed to persuade my sister Simone to join me for a day of blackjack at a casino two hours away in Connecticut. It also happened to be my birthday, so I was happy to have her company. As soon as we arrived at the already busy casino, we grabbed the first vacant seats we could find, and settled into having a good time. After a couple hours, Simone started checking her phone. Naturally, I didn't think anything of it, but when she mentioned wanting to get something to eat, I told her to go without me. Not only was I not hungry, I didn't want to break my standard four-hour block of gambling time and, worse, risk not being able to find another available seat when I got back. So she stayed.

"By the time she mentioned food again an hour or so later, I was ready to take a break. I had worked up enough of an appetite, on top of which I was not doing well that day. Then she added that she wanted Chinese food. I probably reacted with a slight wince at that point. I didn't want to sacrifice too much time at a proper sit-down meal. To make it worse, the large cluster of Chinese restaurants sat at the other end of the casino. So I pointed at the Johnny Rockets restaurant on the way. *Couldn't we just grab a quick burger there?* But she kept at me. Eventually, I gave in and led her to the main food pavilion.

"When we finally arrived, I told her to pick the restaurant she wanted. This time she took the lead and walked into one with an air of certainty. That was when I almost tripped over in shock. There, out of the corner of my eye, sat a familiar sight. I turned to get a better look. I saw my entire family—including Dad. It was the football game all over again. Not only was it a shock to see him in a casino, a place he did not enjoy, it was also my first surprise birthday party. All at once I understood the planning and patience that had gone into making a special moment just for me. Several minutes would pass before I could string a coherent sentence together. I had lost that day at blackjack, but I still left a winner.

"The life lessons continued. As soon as Sabrina and I began working full-time, Dad convinced us to take a chance on a joint real estate investment opportunity he had heard about. He was big on real estate ownership, always telling us: *control your destiny by owning, not renting.* When my sister and I finally agreed to take the plunge, he guided us through the entire process. He took us to the model home, joined us in all our meetings, and even weighed in on which upgrades to take. *Buy quality and you'll only buy it once*, he said. He told us everything to expect—from our respon-sibilities as landlords, to the grab bag of possible tenant surprises.

"I know we were, and continue to be, lucky for his guidance. It's natural as young adults to want to make your own choices, but I'm grateful he offered advice, and relieved we took it. No doubt he saved us from a lot of headaches. I know my dad wants to protect us. I know he wants to make sure we never have to make do with just a single pair of shoes."

Damian HoSang

"Through his signature patience, Dad taught me how to conquer fear and develop a taste for self-reliance.

"I'll never forget the day I finally took the training wheels off my bicycle. All I could focus on was Dad's hands—I wanted them *on* the bicycle. I was petrified I'd go crashing to the ground the second he let go. Dad's voice was like a cool breeze on a warm day. *You'll be fine*, he kept saying. *You'll be OK. Don't be afraid.* With each sentence he spoke, the trust I had in him grew stronger. Before long, his confidence in me cut through my fear. As if sensing it, he let go of the bicycle at precisely that moment. Suddenly, I was riding on my own. I was a whole new person.

"My next wheel-related hurdle came when I was sixteen and learning how to drive. No matter how hard I tried, I couldn't master parallel parking. Dad set up a parking lab by parking two cars on the street—his and Damian's—while I practiced using Mom's car. It was one of those steamy summer days when all you want is the air conditioning on full blast, but I had to have the window down so I could hear his instructions. Dad was about perfection, so half an hour later I was still practicing. That must have led to dehydration, because after a while I began to feel dizzy and disoriented. As I aligned the car parallel to Dad's for what seemed like the fiftieth time, I forgot to shift the car into reverse before stepping on the gas, and drove Mom's car into his. My face in full fright mode, a small freight train ran through my head as I tried to figure out how to explain the accident to her. But I ended up having Dad's company because she got upset with us both. I was so traumatized that only Dad's encouragement got me behind that steering wheel again. A couple weeks later, I aced the test.

"Once I got Damian's old ride, Dad finished his duty by teaching me the nuts and bolts of owning a car. He taught me how to check the oil, check the tire pressure, how to add air, use coins to measure the treading, and even how to deal with a flat. For Dad, it was all about survival training. It was important to him that we knew how to take care of ourselves.

"His philosophy of self-sufficiency also extended to the family business. He always stressed the importance of being a well-rounded business owner open to learning, and always reminded us that hard work was a good teacher. He was also big on candor as a path to a simpler life, even if what you have to say disappoints others. *Get it off your chest*, he'd say. *Not only will you sleep better, you'll be respected for it.*

"I learned more about my father as I got older and began working with him. I saw him to be a true gentleman at his core. He holds doors open for everyone, never lets the lady in his company trail behind him, and offers his seat whether in public or at a private function. No matter who you are, he's always going to give you the better quality item, and take the lesser quality one for himself. Today, when I step through the door at work, I view him as a business partner—as Mr. HoSang. At home, however, he's still the father who used to hoist me on his shoulders for piggyback rides. At home, he's 'Dad.'"

Sabrina HoSang Jordan

"When we were kids, my baby brother, Brian, and I used to go to Dyre after school and share half a dozen cocktail patties. Once we were a little older and could see just over the table, we started working at the Mount Vernon plant. Our job was to squish the balls of dough for the coco bread. At Tappan, we got promoted to box assembly, which we did while singing to each other, alternating verses of whatever our current favorite song was. No question about it—the family business was like a family member.

"'If you don't take care of the business, it won't take care of you,' is what my dad would always say. That philosophy both ruled and rewarded us. It meant not always having our parents around when we wanted them, and missing out on certain things—like summer camp—because you were expected to spend holidays at the business. Naturally, we didn't understand the sacrifices being made for us. We worried about other things—like trying to be like all the other Westchester kids who had cool pizza parties for their birthdays. Instead, our birthday parties always involved a huge Jamaican-style buffet. To her credit, Mom did take a few years off to look after us until we were all in high school, and she did eventually let me go to summer camp the last year I was eligible.

"But, while I didn't understand the sacrifices, I knew that the business was the reason behind our comfortable life. Our parents' siblings benefitted too. Some lived with us until they could stand on their own (which is why Sabrina and I cook in large volumes). We even helped some of our cousins with their college tuition. Dad didn't want any of us dropping out of school because of a lack of money. He was proud he could provide so well for the family. I saw that.

"He wasn't all about work, though. He liked to see us have fun. I'll never forget the time he got us a BB gun and set up a shooting range in the basement. We were so excited. My brothers went first. Then it was my turn. I positioned myself the way I'd seen them do it in the movies, and pulled the trigger. Not only did I completely miss the target, but I also shot a perfect hole in the window. I remember Dad's eyes growing wide. 'Ah…OK,' he said, 'I'll…I'll take care of it. Just *don't* tell your mother.' That was Dad. He always had our backs. I remember once wanting to go on the really big slide during one of our water park outings. Dad waited with me in the long line that snaked up the stairs. But the closer we got to the top, the more scared I became. When it was my turn, I froze and shook my head. Dad simply smiled, took my hand, and walked back down with me.

"As we grew older, he was still there, watching out for us. I was fifteen when I went to my first dance club. I remember the moment the bouncer's flashlight got me in the face. 'Time to go, kid' he said. 'Your father's here.' The second time I went, Dad actually went inside to check the place out. He didn't like it, of course, and told me so, but didn't ban me from going. He let us be kids.

"When I got my first job outside of the family business, he gave me this speech about not taking money out of the cash register. 'The owner has worked hard for every penny,' he said. 'You must respect that.' At first I was shocked that he felt it necessary to even say that. Then I realized that it wasn't about me but about what he'd had to endure to build his business.

"Saving was another favorite topic of his. He shared lots of stories to make the lesson stick, including tales about watching friends spend their hard-earned money at bars. Those same friends would end up asking for his help later on. While at college, I had a part-time job, first at Boston Market, and at then a midtown restaurant. Sure enough, my coworkers were always inviting me out. I'd tag along and watch them spend almost a third—if not all—of what they had just worked so hard on their feet to earn that night.

"I'm grateful that my father's lessons registered early in my life. While he wanted to give us everything, he also wanted us to learn important life skills. When he had me take out my first car loan, for instance, it was to teach me not just how to establish good credit, but how to take on responsibilities. He's big on that. Even though he emphasizes philanthropy and kindness, his big wish for us is self-reliance. 'Don't depend on others,' he tells us. 'Learn as much as you can, try to make good choices and, above all, live life with a positive attitude.'

"It's different growing up knowing that your parents have created a business for you to step into. On the one hand, you know they're hoping you'll eventually take the baton. On the other, you have your own dreams. I had always been good at art, something my parents encouraged. I explored that path by taking classes at the Fashion Institute of Technology. One of my courses was the Business of Fashion. One day, they hosted a guest speaker from a top name in fashion. I shared my story with the class, telling them that my father worried about the life of a starving artist, and wanted me to get a degree in food science so I could work for the business. *I*, however, wanted to do fashion design.

"I thought I was going to get a rousing cheer of support. After all, we were there for our love of fashion. I will never forget the speaker's reply. 'Your dad is right,' he said. 'Do you know how lucky you are? Do you know how many people would love to be in your shoes? This is an incredibly competitive business. I suggest you work in the family business and do fashion as a hobby. If you find you're still passionate about it, nothing will stop you from working in that field.' That day, I went home and told Dad about the speaker's advice. He smiled with a relieved twinkle in his eye. 'Good,' he said. 'I'm happy you heard it from someone else, too.'"

Simone HoSang

We were now settled in Pleasantville, smiling each time we pulled into the generous driveway of our new home.

Then, in 1990, I got the call I'd been waiting for. It was the realtor with news of a factory available in Tappan, New York. A former machine factory in excellent shape, the plant was less than half an hour's drive away from our new home. For that reason alone, I liked it already. When I asked Bill for the square footage, my question was met with a long pause. Then my realtor's voice returned. It was 73,000 square feet of factory space sprawled across ten acres of land.

It was my turn to go silent. Swallowing a deep breath, I told him I was ready to hear the asking price. His answer made it even harder. Already in receivership, the bank was asking for $2.5 million—given the size and condition of the property, it was a steal. When he gave me the ballpark figure for the property taxes, however, he may as well have doused me with ice-cold water. I had never paid that kind of taxes before.

My heart sank. For perhaps only the second time in my life, I heard myself say the word *no. That's too much,* I told myself, and my realtor. *I can't do that.*

A week passed. Feeling uncharacteristically deterred but decidedly curious, I went to see the place. I had to admit—it was like setting eyes on the flashiest car in the showroom. Still reeling from the prohibitive tax commitment, however, I told my realtor that this prize was way out of my league. It was bad enough that I could see us making Jamaican patties day after day in all that incredible space—tens of thousands of patties. The leap of faith it required was, however, too much, even for me. We held tight at Mount Vernon while we kept on looking.

A year went by. Still on the market, the Tappan factory sat quietly at the back of my mind. Then, early one morning while having my coffee in my office, I decided to put numbers to paper. I let the math do the talking and faith do the listening.

That's when it all became clear. I saw that if we could, at a minimum, do the same numbers at Tappan in 73,000 square feet that we were already doing at Mount Vernon in 20,000, we could actually meet our financial obligations. My heart jumped. Between my determination and our dedicated team, I knew we could knock those numbers out of the park.

Hope surged in me, practically lifting me out of my chair. I grabbed the phone to call Bill, my realtor, to confirm that Tappan was back on the table. First, however, I needed him to find out what the current asking price was. A lot could change in a year. I didn't have to wait long for him to call back with the good news. The bank was still willing to offload the property for the same song: $2.5 million. I threw my head back in disbelief. Tappan had been waiting on us the entire time, waiting for me to see the light. I could hardly believe it.

In late 1992, Tappan officially became ours. The next year and a half saw us enduring yet another expansion marathon. Once again, we filed the requisite papers, secured the necessary loans, and wrestled through the renovations. Meanwhile, life continued as it always does even when you're juggling a few fires. In March of 1993, at the age of seventy-seven, Uncle Harrison passed away. I flew to Montego Bay for the funeral. Standing beside Aunt Sylvia, I tried to make peace with the only regret I had about him. I never did tell him how he had shaped me. Sometimes, we Chinese can be opaque, frugal with even our words. As his coffin sat at the front of the church, I thought back to the day I left his house and shop to be reunited with my parents. I saw Ahshook's face again the moment he looked away, and remembered the silence that followed. His look of disappointment had never left my mind. Then I remembered my promise to make it up to him one day. So, immediately after the funeral, I took over the financial wellbeing of his widow. As the union had produced no children of their own, I would take care of my second mother in honor of the man who had once accepted his role as my second father.

In 1994, Caribbean Food Delights moved into its Tappan home, and began operating under the watchful eye of our brand new, and much more agreeable, USDA inspector. It was my regret that neither of my two fathers could have been there to see what fruit their combined lessons had produced.

CHAPTER 17

It is in the giving that we receive

"When you look back on your life and path to success, acknowledge those who helped you along the way. Once you're in a position to do so, honor their kindness by paying it forward."

Vincent

SINCE THE DAY WE SIGNED THE PURCHASE AGREE-ment for the Tappan plant in 1992, life shifted into high gear. I had always seen growth in our future, but never did I imagine this. We were now operating in 73,000 square feet of factory. I believed then, as I do now, that all we had accomplished was by the will of God. I was merely following what I sensed to be His directions. My thank-you prayers got longer each morning as the list of blessings grew, so I made sure to also thank Him for my strong knees.

As if heralding a new avenue in my life, I began to meet more individuals with whom I'd forge close bonds. These were, and continue to be, genuine friendships for which I am blessed. It's not often that a man can count on more than one hand the number of friends ready to help in an emergency. One such friend was a holy man with whom, unbeknownst to us both, I shared a family connection:

> "When I was stationed in Montego Bay, I became friendly with a member of the congregation, one Mrs. Sylvia Ho. A talented baker and cook, Sylvia ended up baking for my wife and me, our first wedding anniversary cake. And it was at Sylvia's restaurant that I had lunch almost daily. When, in 1990, it came time for us to relocate to New York, she mentioned that she had a son in that city.

> "Well it didn't take us long to cross paths with said son. At a 1992 function in Brooklyn, this Chinese gentleman came up and introduced himself. On hearing that I hailed from Montego Bay, he told me that his mother, Sylvia Ho, lived there. I broke into a smile. 'But that's *my* mother!' I said. 'She fed me almost every day! So *you're* the son she told me to look out for!' We agreed that as the

same 'mother' had nourished us, we would be, not just friends, but brothers too.

"Our bond cemented from there. Vinnie began asking me to emcee his company's annual staff appreciation dinners. When I was having something at my church, he'd be on the phone offering his help. In fact, when I was made rector of the Church of the Good Shepherd, he came to my rescue when I realized that more people were attending the installation than the church could hold. This meant moving it to the Cathedral of St. John the Divine, even though I was not the rector there. The problem doubled when we realized that there was no facility in which to heat the meal being served at the repast. That's when Vinnie uttered the words now almost synonymous with him: 'I can help with that.' And, so, he offered a food truck he had gotten specially made to help at charity events.

"From there it just snowballed. When my church needed an organ, he was the first to give me a check for over a couple thousand dollars. When I needed a bus for the church to pick up our seniors, again he appeared with an even larger contribution. He does more than just cut a check, too—he shows up. I could merely mention in passing that I'm about to visit friends out of state, and suddenly he's at my door with a box of frozen patties that he packed himself, or loaves of bread and bun for me to take as gifts. There he is, the head of a huge company, delivering it himself, with no expectations of anything in return. He is simply not impressed by his success.

"In time, I learned that he stands by his motto: *It is in the giving that I receive.* I'll never forget the day I called Vinnie with a real SOS. It had to do with a young lady who had recently graduated from the teacher's college in Kingston, Jamaica. Trying to stand on her own, she had taken out a bank loan. Unable to secure a job after graduation, she had failed to make her loan payments. Now the bank was taking legal action. She called me on the morning she was due to appear in court. 'Father Mac,' she gasped in between sobs, 'after today I'm sure you won't want to be associated with me. After today, I'll be in prison.'

"Needless to say I was frightened for this young lady, whom I had helped before. Since I had just finished paying my own bills, however, I was short of extra cash in that quantity. Desperate to help her, I immediately called the one person I knew who would not hesitate to help a stranger with a legitimate problem. I didn't know if or how Vincent could get the money to her within the hour from New York, but I knew he would not stop until he had tried everything possible.

"Vinnie's phone rings no matter where he is. You can count on him to answer, even if it's to say that he has to call you back. Even though I had called this man hundreds of times before, hearing him answer that day was like stirring a pack of hot chocolate into a mug of hot water—it gave me instant hope. 'Vinnie, it's Father Mac. I need your help urgently.' After explaining the impossible situation, there was a short pause followed by a burst of laughter. I was startled.

"'What…*why* are you laughing?' I asked.

"'Because I'm in Kingston.'

I joined in with my own hearty laughter. Within the hour, he was in contact with the young lady as she made her way to the courthouse, and pressing into her palms the money she needed. Thanks to Vincent's swift action, and to the Lord who put His faithful servant in the right place at the right time, prison never saw that young miss for even a second.

"She's just one of numerous students he's helped. His company's scholarship fund has helped many youngsters find their way through college. None of this is a surprise to those who know him well.

It's why we believe him when he says that the more he makes is the more he can help. That's Vinnie HoSang—when he tells you he's going to do something, it's already done."

Rev. Canon Calvin McIntyre
Rector, Church of the
Good Shepherd

In January of 1994, I got a call from a young fellow I'd see occasionally at various community functions. Irwine G. Clare, Sr. wanted to speak with me about helping the Jamaican participants in the upcoming Penn Relays. I had already heard of the efforts made by others in the immediate area to house the athletes during their visit. As it was, most could barely scrape together the airfare. Food and lodging were extra comforts they could only hope to find once here. So when I got the call from Irwine, I didn't hesitate to meet.

Still completing the final touches at the Tappan plant, I arranged for his presentation to take place at Mount Vernon. I was looking forward to meeting with young Clare. I liked his high energy and enthusiasm. However, as I was still licking my wounds from the recent ambushing by my project manager and engineer, I did not trust myself to go into these new talks alone. So, I called someone with much more experience at negotiating. Myrna Merchant was a lovely lady and formidable professional. A career banker, over the years she had become a loyal customer and true friend. So when I asked her to sit in as my reinforcement, she was only too happy to oblige.

Only a fool feigns expertise. The true leader admits to his or her limitations, brings in the experts, then steps back to watch and learn.

When Irwine arrived with his associate that Friday, I apologized for the cramped space, but assured them that our next meeting would be in a larger, more comfortable conference room:

> "Up to this point, I had only spoken with Vinnie socially, but always felt at ease. His aura is one of benevolence. Most people talk *at* you only so that they can talk about themselves. Not Vinnie. He doesn't just hear you, he sees you. He connects with what you're saying. You sense that you can depend on him.
>
> "I still remember that Friday evening in Vinnie's Mount Vernon conference room. As a result of its size and orientation, my friend and I ended up stuck in the corner. Unless we literally stepped over Mr. HoSang and his 'treasury guard,' Myrna Merchant, there was no way out. We were trapped. I don't think it was intentional on Mr. HoSang's part, to be honest. It just happened that way. But, coming out of corporate America, I understood the strategies used in negotiations and quickly

noted our disadvantage. I knew that the only way out was to be successful.

"With apprehension underscored by excitement, I proceeded with my carefully rehearsed presentation. For some reason, I suddenly became terribly verbose. I just kept talking and talking while Vinnie listened and listened. But each time I delivered a point he seemed to be comfortable with, Ms. Merchant sent it through the shredder. If I explained that two plus two equaled four, she showed me that it equaled *negative* four. A banker with a prominent commercial bank at the time, the lady was not to be played with. That much was clear.

"After a few tough rounds, however, a sudden fearlessness washed over me, as if a higher power had stepped in. I kept at it. Vinnie was professional and respectful. His eyes never looked elsewhere in boredom or distraction. In the end, he saw that our intentions were genuine. It was not about Irwine Clare earning a penny from this, but about helping kids who were reaching for the stars. It was about empowering a community. As we rose from the table, we shook hands on his commitment to provide lunch for the athletes.

"Vinnie likes to say that he started out with a 'little patty shop.' We had a similar beginning with him and the Penn Relays. At first he drove down to Philadelphia in a small panel van filled with his patties and breads and some juices. I don't mean that he had it driven down by one of his workers. No. The man sat behind the wheel, put his own foot on the gas pedal, and made the six-hour-long return trip himself.

"That small van evolved into a thirty-foot by sixty-foot tent, complete with generator and other appliances that allow for onsite cooking of hot, plated meals. Today, in addition to providing the athletes with a cafeteria on wheels, he faithfully hands over a check for ten thousand dollars to help offset accommodation expenses.

"That's why I maintain that while Vinnie HoSang may be a small and simple man, he has a big heart and an even bigger shadow. He may not say much, nor does he speak loudly, but he makes things happen. He shows up, literally rolls up his sleeves, sweeps the tent, serves the food, and takes orders from the organizers as if he were hired help.

"To this day, as successful as he is, he still makes time for thoughtfulness. If I didn't know it then, I knew it the day I met him in Kingston for yet another athletic event. Somehow I had inveigled him to attend the iconic Boys and Girls Champs. So there I was, relaxing in the lobby of one of the city's nicer hotels, when I see Vinnie coming through the door and walking my way with his usual smile. He had just arrived from Montego Bay after spending a little time fishing with his brother King. His suitcase looked like something out of the seventies—one of those hard tan cases with the stickers all over it. I chuckled. It was so like him.

"Well, the smiles didn't end there. After we greet one another, lo and behold, he drops the suitcase on the floor, cracks it open, and starts whipping out an entire cafeteria: bun from his bakery, coconut water from his brother George's farm, and fried Barracuda from his fishing expedition. Fried barracuda! At that point the laughter just erupted out of me. I couldn't stop. That's classic Vinnie—he just wants to make you happy.

"Every now and then the dictionary is updated. I wouldn't be surprised if one day I looked up the word *philanthropist*, and saw *Vinnie HoSang* listed as a new synonym."

Irwine G. Clare, Sr., O.D. Jamaica
Team Jamaica Bickle

Our involvement with the Penn Relays marked the start of an annual pilgrimage of sorts for me. There is nothing quite like the rush of helping others achieve their goals. I admire those young athletes. They throw their talent and passion at life with faith and hope, but harbor no sense of entitlement. The fact that there can only be one winner does not stop them from trying. They remind me of my early days as an immigrant, when I had no time for fear or self-pity.

I discovered the similarity between us the day one of the athletes personally thanked me for our help. As sometimes happens with Caribbean children when addressing adults, he avoided making eye contact, instead, stealing shy glances now and then. In a soft voice, he shared the past experience of having to sleep at the stadium because there was no money for a room. I winced at the thought of those kids sleeping on the cold concrete.

The youngster stopped me as I began to express sympathy. Suddenly, his white teeth appeared behind a reassuring smile. With our help added to the contributions of others, he said, they could now rest in warm beds, eat hot meals, and give the relays their best. He just wanted to thank me in person for removing the worry from the experience. I was never more impressed. He wasn't asking for sympathy—for that, I gave him my respect. Each year, I clear my calendar for the Penn Relays. I want to make sure I'm there to cheer these champions on.

A few years later, in 1998, I met Jamaica's new Consul General to New York, Dr. Basil Bryan. Previously stationed in Washington, DC, as the deputy ambassador, the tall and stately Dr. Bryan was every bit the quintessential diplomat. He, too, was another gentleman whom I would soon call *friend*:

"From time to time I'd come across Vincent HoSang's name and that of his companies through the media or conversations with others. I can't recall our first meeting, but I do recall that my first impression was of his singular humility. There are no airs about him. You sense this immediately on shaking his hand.

"After settling down in my new post, it didn't take long for me to understand that Vincent was a significant part of the community outreach landscape. If there was a cause that needed attention, he was there—time, talent, and treasure. Not once did he make me feel as if I was imposing on him. If he had donor fatigue, he never showed it. In fact, sometimes he would call me before I even had the chance to dial his number, asking me about plans I had in place concerning a particular situation or the other. The phone would ring and there he was, ready to help: 'What do you need? What can I do?'

"That was certainly the case when Hurricane Katrina hit the coast of New Orleans. We knew that the hospitality guest workers would be among those affected, especially as most had no family or friends in the area for support. Our goal was to work with our contacts in Houston to help relocate them from the New Orleans and Mississippi coastlines. Mr. HoSang was one of the few business owners from a distance offering help. There was no cutting of ribbons, no displaying of company banners, no coverage by the media of this behind-the-scenes rescue mission. Nothing.

"He gets great joy from lifting up the disadvantaged. It's the reason I recommended him in 2002 as a recipient of the Order of Distinction, a national order in Jamaica's honor system. I said to myself, *This man must be recognized publicly by his country of origin. He deserves it.* Not surprisingly, he took it all in stride. He merely smiled and said he would accept the honor for those he had helped.

"Vincent does his best to instill in his children the same concern for the poor. His kids are American-born, of course, so it's a little harder for them to connect with the extreme poverty of their parents' homeland. They won't have the benefit of the attachment and deep-seated heartache we feel, but you always see one or all of them with him as he tends to his many charities both in the States and abroad. They are wonderful children.

"Father Richard Ho Lung has made the observation that there is something to be said about the mixture of the Chinese and the Jamaican. As he puts it, exceptions aside, the Chinese individual generally tends to be low-key and modest, while the Jamaican revels in excitement and achievements, and is highly emotional. I have always thought this to be a unique part of our culture. You could even make the argument that they are polar opposites. Vincent is a nice combination of both. He achieves quietly, but I've seen him enjoy himself on the dance floor, too, with that smile of his."

Dr. Basil Bryan, O.D., Jamaica

Even though I was part of the early wave of Jamaicans to leave the island's shores, I never forgot my promise to remain close. When you've taken your first breaths in a land so breathtaking, it's hard to imagine your life without it, but my land of birth is a living paradox—it soothes your soul with its God-given beauty, and crushes it with its perpetual challenges.

Jamaica has varying degrees of poverty: from gentle scarcity to outright destitution. Struggles abound. Lucky breaks are rare. Having family there made it easier for me to keep a watchful eye on the island's progress, or lack thereof. We continued to reach out as best we could. Sometimes we helped in small ways, while other times we gave more significantly. Through a connection made socially, in 2002 we became the proud benefactors of the endowment of the HoSang Entrepreneurship Programme at the University of the West Indies, Mona campus. We could think of no better way to applaud the university's culture of entrepreneurship. Our support remains to this day.

I hold in high esteem those who awaken each day to make the lives of others a little more bearable. My sister-in-law Carmen, King's wife, was the first to tell me about the unparalleled work of the incredible Father Richard Ho Lung. When I heard of the Jesuit priest's devotion, not just to the poor, but to the poorest of the poor—the forgotten—I felt at once compelled to call him:

> "After my childhood friend Carmen told Vincent about the Brothers and our work in Jamaica, he simply opened himself up to us: 'Father, my name is Vincent HoSang,' he said, his calm but eager voice streaming through the phone. 'I love the work you're doing in Jamaica with Missionaries of the Poor. I'd like to help you. Please tell me how.' Well my goodness, since that day, he's been wonderful. Because of his kindness, we've been able to expand our homes in Jamaica for the destitute and homeless.

"I first met him in person when he came to present us with his generous check. I have to say that I was completely surprised by his simplicity. I couldn't understand how such a simple man could achieve so much without becoming proud. I was also immediately struck by the way he balances his Chinese and Jamaican heritages. The Chinese part of him is understated, cheerful, and without any brag at all. Then he has this other side of being a rooted Jamaican: practical, positive, rarely self-sympathetic, equipped with a great deal of common sense. He also has that signature Jamaican fearlessness—the same fortitude behind so many creative ventures, like our bobsled team. Vincent has that daring and courage to try. Try, he did. Succeed, he did.

"Since that first meeting, the relationship has continued. I've found that he has not a rambunctious humor, but a kind of inner smile that radiates. He has told me about his simple country life and his life in the Chinese store. He laughs at himself that way. It's almost as if he's still surprised that, despite the lack of much formal education and training, God chose to dispense on him a wonderful, sensible approach to life. It is as if he and the Lord have this little relationship, and the Lord is playing with him.

"It is a deep, informal faith with Vincent, not a fashion statement. So rooted is it in him, that he has a kind of brotherly quality about him. He truly sees himself as better than no one else in this world."

Very Rev. Fr. Richard Ho Lung
Founder, Missionaries of the
Poor, MOP

I believe in charity. The way I see it, we don't get to live forever, and we don't get to take it with us. I believe in my heart that the Lord wants me to be successful, not just so I can help my own family, but His too. I think of that just about every morning I walk through my factory's doors, put on my hairnet and gown, and begin my day.

CHAPTER 18

My *"Jamerican"* pie

"When it comes to making business projections, be cautiously optimistic. Projections are not promises. They are merely your most educated guess based on your past performance, your current costs, and your sales forecast, itself also a projection."

Vincent

IT WAS 1994. TAPPAN, NEW YORK WAS NOW HOME to our new factory. While the vast space meant more monster machines, even more complicated renovations, and massive loans, this time there were no rogue waves that had me reaching for beer in the mornings. I was back to basic coffee. We had finally arrived at that certain sweet spot—where hard-won experience translated into smoother sailing.

Exhausted but energized, we had thrown a wonderful affair for the official grand opening, and invited as many family and friends as we could. Everyone cheered us on with love and admiration. Up to that point, most had only heard about what we were doing. Seeing it, however, was a completely different matter. Eyes widened and mouths fell open as we took our visitors around for the tour. A couple well-meaning friends couldn't contain their concern for me. I got comments like:

"Vinnie! How are you going to manage all this?"

"Vinnie, what will you do if it doesn't work?"

"I'm going to pray for you, my friend. I'm going to pray hard!"

I could only chuckle at their sincere shock and genuine happiness. I'd have said the same things had I been the one watching his close friend take a cliff dive. I didn't show bravado, though. I didn't wave them off with a breezy and dismissive "everything's gonna be all right." I told them the truth—that I had no choice but to make it work. If I didn't, I was going to be in a lot of trouble, so I encouraged them to pray for me.

My brother King had also made the trip for our big day. He smiled quietly the entire time, his eyes doing most of the talking. I was incredibly grateful that he was there to share in the moment. King had been with me all along. My brother and

I didn't say much to one another that day, but we didn't have to. I know that we were both thinking of our Springfield days.

Jeanie was by my side, of course. Our four children, now no longer babies, were also there to help us celebrate. They had long become their own personalities, and a source of deep pride and delight to us. Damian, seventeen and surprisingly tall, was already a college student. Sabrina was fifteen and still in high school. Thirteen-year-old Simone and eleven-year-old Brian were both in middle school. Each had been brought up in the business from an early age so that they would know some of the basics. At the very least, I wanted to make sure they got a feel for the kind of business we had built.

As they got older and more involved in school and their own lives, I left it to each to decide how much time he or she wished to devote to the family business. As much as I wanted to instill a strong work ethic in my children, I also did not want to be a demanding parent. All I could do was hope that we had built something they were proud of—proud enough to want to join in a leadership capacity. If it turned out that their talents and desires took them in another direction, I would have been fine with that. So, I left the door wide open. I had been left alone to choose my path in life, so I would give them the same consideration.

Production resumed before the last balloon from the festivities had been pulled down. Sales with our established customers continued to climb. Now backed by a real capacity for production, I found a sales manager with experience to match, and set him loose on the field.

Meanwhile, I began to quietly act on an idea I had been toying with for some time. We had already sold our customers on our patty's great taste. Now it was time to add another ingredient to its allure: convenience. I knew the patty had the potential to become the next crossover ethnic fast food in convenience-hungry America. If we could give the consumer a patty that went from frozen to hot on their plate in minutes, we stood a chance at putting a small dent in the mainstream market. All we had to do was take an old favorite and give it a new twist. I acknowledged, with a wry smile, that my plan would probably make most Jamaicans faint. For most die-hards, a patty can only emerge from an oven, plain and simple. With an eye on the future, I began planning for the world's first microwavable patty.

After locating a source for the microwavable paper and making the requisite changes to our production line, we had our modern-day *Jamerican* pie. Packaging them in twos, eights, and eventually tens, our sales manager got us through the doors and on the shelves of BJ's Wholesale Club and Costco. The Jamaican patty had finally entered the mainstream market and new millennium. That day, I gave God one of my longest prayers of gratitude.

Feeling more bullish than ever about our future, I added more muscle to our workforce. We had approximately fifty workers coming through our doors each day. It was a small number, but I was proud of each job we had created. There is no greater feeling than knowing your actions have translated into something positive in the lives of others.

I interacted with our people as I had from the beginning. I worked alongside them wherever I could, inquired about their day, their families and more. By this time, several had come to me with their personal concerns, particularly those of the financial kind. I knew most of our workers by name, and took our extremely low turnover rate as a sign of their overall contentment. Which is why, when on September 14, 1998, our workforce went on strike, I felt as if I had just sauntered into a glass door.

Higher wages was the bone of contention. Yet, not only had I stayed on top of wage increases, I had already extended certain benefits I considered important to our workers' quality of life, including health care. I can only assume that our workers felt entitled to more, now that we were a bigger company. At Tappan, only some workers took restive action. Mount Vernon was hardest hit. Although it was the smaller location, with only fifteen employees, almost all joined the strike.

There are two reasons why we were able to continue production at Mount Vernon: Lalta Singh and Barry Evans. Lalta was one of our mechanics. He was not in favor of the strike. A multi-talented fellow and incredible worker, he said, "Boss, I can do everything in this plant, except mix, so if you can get someone to do that, I'll take care of the rest." Barry was a close friend and young entrepreneur with his own busy bakery in Queens. He offered help by way of two of his workers and himself. They took care of the mixing and worked around Lalta. I jumped in to help with production. When I wasn't baking, I was delivering. Fortunately, I had kept my commercial driver's license current after my milkman days. With the help of a neighborhood police officer who offered his time while off-duty, I even hauled our garbage from the Mount Vernon plant. Sadly, Barry's life was cut short by cancer, not long after the strike. I was blessed to have had his and Lalta's support. It did not come at their convenience, but with considerable sacrifice.

I won't deny that, as a family, we took the strike personally. It was impossible to hide our disappointment and frustration, especially when the concept of being unproductive did not sit well with me. How ironic, I said to myself, that I crossed a picket line on my first day as an employee back in Jamaica. I had done it, not out of insensitivity, but out of respect for the owners' investment. Now, here I was with a strike on my own hands. I wondered whether I had tried to do too much too soon for my staff. My attempt to emulate the big boys—the Arnold and Wonder Bread companies—had backfired on me. My staff deserved the best, but I also deserved to give myself a fighting chance at the front end.

One day, as she was coming into work at the Tappan plant, my daughter stopped to speak with one of the protestors. Sabrina did not recognize her as one of our workers, and so concluded that she was either a customer or general sympathizer. With a respectful smile, Sabrina asked if she could see the sheet of paper the lady and the others were holding, but the lady recognized her and refused. She shouted at Sabrina about getting her own flyer, and taking better care of our workers. Incensed, Sabrina walked away in silence. Then, just as she was going through the door, she turned to the lady and shook her head. "You don't know *half* the things we do to help our people!"

Work resumed that December amid tension. I found it hard to return to business as usual. It felt a bit like having an argument with a friend. You don't assume that every day is going to be a bed of roses. You'll have disagreements, but to take such definitive action against your employer is to cross a certain line. It requires patience and understanding to move on. Fortunately, I had both in spades.

That summer, I would meet another important addition to our growing company. My entire family, production manager, Charles, and I had decided to attend a Hazard Analysis Critical Control Point conference ("HACCP"). Amid the large gathering of food producers milling about, Charles had the good fortune of meeting a young food science professional from the Philippines by the name of Raquel Pascual. Armed with her university degree, she had come to America in 1994, determined to make a better life. At first taking housekeeping jobs, she eventually made her way back to her field. She reminded me a lot of another fellow we had hired. Napoleon was a ship's mechanic who had also come to the United States in search of hope. Armed with a firm resolve and stellar attitude to match, he told us everything we needed to know when he answered one particular question on our job application form.

The question: "What position are you seeking with our company?"

His answer: "Anything."

We hired him on the spot.

If this young lady was anything like Napoleon (who also hailed from the Philippines), we were definitely impressed and interested. After asking Raquel a few questions, Charles casually threw out the suggestion that she come work for us as our food science manager, and signaled for me to come meet her. I could tell by the way he was gesticulating that he had found us a good prospect. Now that we were a larger company with several production lines on the go, we needed someone with her particular expertise. Unfortunately, she was already employed elsewhere. That small detail, however, would soon sort itself out a few months later.

> "When I first met Mr. HoSang, his warmth came through his smile and immediately put me at ease. He asked lots of questions, practically interviewing me on the spot. I was most impressed at how hands-on the entire family was. Instead of sending a representative as my then-employer had done, they all came themselves. At the end

of our chat, he gave me his card and asked me to call if I ever found a food science professional for him. I guess God had a plan for me. Even though I was happy with my job, something told me to keep his card.

"In a twist of fate, I found out that December that my company was relocating to Vermont. My job was secure. The problem was I didn't want to move. There was my husband and his job to consider, as well as another problem. Newly pregnant with my first child, I was experiencing a high-risk pregnancy, which required bed rest. To complicate matters, I was in the United States on a work visa. Overwhelmed, I went to my Rolodex and found Mr. HoSang's card. As I dialed his number, I prayed that he would remember me. I needn't have worried.

"'Did you find someone for me?' he chimed at the other end of the phone. Relieved that the position was still available, I told him I had, and that I was the candidate. 'Great!' he returned. 'Come in and let's talk!' Nervous, but wanting to put it all out on the table, I explained the issues with my pregnancy and visa. He hired me right away, despite the fact that I could not take up my position until after I had delivered my baby, and despite the fact that he would have to take over my sponsorship. I had been handed a gift. Not for one moment did he make me feel small or indebted for the patience and effort required on his part, not even when my start date was further thwarted by kidney failure after my delivery. He just seemed to understand that, sometimes, life just goes wrong.

"He came to visit me at the hospital the day before my kidney transplant. Worried about my baby, my health, and my job, I was crying. 'Don't worry about your job,' he whispered as he walked with me to my sister's room across the hall—she was my kidney donor. 'Focus on your health. Your transplant will go well and your job will be waiting for you.' There he was, barely my new boss, and already he's taking the time, not just to visit, but also to give me peace of mind. That kind man ended up waiting eighteen months before I could begin working—an entire year and a half. I knew then that I had chosen well.

"Bosses come in different packages. Mr. HoSang is the kind who sees us as people, not just people who work for him. One day, one of my staff members came to me with a personal problem. Her landlord had given her an eviction notice of only one week. While she had managed to find a new place in that short time, she didn't have the security deposit, plus first and last month's rent. I went to Mr. HoSang. Without hesitation, he helped her out. But he does more than solve problems. He counsels too. If someone makes a mistake on the job, he doesn't yell. He talks. He calmly asks the person, 'OK, what happened?' and gives him or her a chance to explain. He'll do everything to avoid writing someone up. For him, it's all about having a good attitude. If you can give him that, he'll give you his patience and respect. He'll give you that chance to prove yourself.

"I know this is where I belong. I've had other generous job offers since joining the company, but I understand the value of what I have. It's not always about money. It's also about relationships. Because of Mr. HoSang, I have learned to better appreciate what God has given me, including the privilege of living in this country."

Raquel Pascual
Food Technologist
Caribbean Food Delights

Like so many others here—from our sales and marketing team to administration and production—Raquel has our company's best interest at heart. She'll come in earlier than she needs to, be the last to leave, and even wash the floors if she feels they weren't done properly. I treasure those who give more than expected: the ones who stay behind that extra half hour to accommodate a late customer pickup; the ones who suggest improvements, even if it's outside of their department. Thanks to my staff's dedication, the company would go on to earn level three SQF status ("Safe Quality Food") in 2011, the highest ranking possible in the United States.

The stronger my team got, the more confident I felt about our future. Not to be left out was the "keeper" of our accounts—the protector of every company's underbelly. As our bankers required us to have an outside accounting officer, we went looking for that perfect fit. Not only were we hunting for a firm with experience in the food and manufacturing sectors, we wanted a certain comfort level—professional chemistry. We took our time sifting through a number of quality firms with brilliant CPAs. I first met Brad Kreinces at our Tappan office:

"Going into the meeting, I had learned what I could about my prospective client from his banker, but it never came up that Vincent was a Jamaican businessman of Chinese descent. So when we shook hands and he began to speak, his accent caused me to do a double take. I had never encountered Chinese-Jamaicans before, so it took me a minute to digest this intriguing combination. I tried my hardest not to appear unnerved.

"With his controller explaining the company's needs and plans, we got off to a great start. There was this natural give-and-take synergy, which led to our eventual engagement by the company. Since then, I've gotten to know its founder and CEO well. I've heard several refer to him as 'lucky.' Yes, everyone needs a bit of luck to be successful. Luck, however, implies a passive involvement, as if the individual is merely riding a wave. After years of working with, and observing, him, I can say that Vincent is anything but passive when it comes to his family, workers, business, and charities. 'Lucky' describes those who have flashes of success in an otherwise mediocre career. Vincent's consistent—almost flawless—string of successes, some of which were made against the odds, proves that he is the real deal. Baseball is a great analogy for the life of an entrepreneur—as a player you're going to have strikeouts, foul balls, and little dribblers to the pitcher. Vincent regularly hits doubles, triples, and home runs. He is a true entrepreneur.

"In our profession, we joke that if it were up to advisors to take risks, the business world would be plain vanilla because we prefer to play it safe. Vincent pushes the envelope, takes calculated risks, makes sure he understands potential consequences, and decides where to turn at crossroads. When he first came to the United States, he took relatively small risks that were large relative to his life. That remains his business model to this day.

"Without a doubt, he exhibits all the traits I've come to admire about successful people. He encounters hurdles, like all business owners do, but is not a head-in-the-sand kind of guy. He addresses the problem, resolves it, and then moves on. The secret is that he is both street and people smart. In every meeting, for instance, he'll encourage and entertain differing opinions on a particular subject. At some point, however, he'll put his stamp on it. That's when you'll hear him say, 'OK, based on all these great points, this is what we're going to do.'

"What's really amazing is that, despite his company's size, he's managed to maintain this comfortable family environment. Not only does he communicate well with his team, he makes them part of his company's evolution by giving them the autonomy with which to perform their duties. It is both instinctive and smart. For that, his team consistently rewards him with respect, loyalty, and great results."

Brad Kreinces, CPA, CGMA
Kreinces Rollins & Shanker, LLC

Brad came into our lives in 2000, and became part of the core team. I am a blessed man a hundred times over for the people I now have around me—they are champions. It is a privilege to work with others who not only share your vision for the future, but also the same excitement. They make me look forward to walking through our doors every day.

A year later, on September 11, 2001, I found myself in Vegas at another bakery convention in search of more machines for the Tappan plant. Jeanie and Damian were with me. Grief and disbelief struck our hearts as we learned about the horror unfolding in New York City. By lunchtime, organizers had cancelled the convention. Guests scrambled around, stress drawn across their faces as they tried to make it out of Vegas. Particularly panicked were those of us from the New York and tristate area. With all planes grounded, most people turned to renting cars. When those were all gone, some guests took to pooling together to *buy* cars.

My family and I decided to wait it out. Two days later, we boarded a flight. We arrived to find a city deep in shock, but steeped in resolve to heal and rise again. I was never more proud to be a New Yorker.

As we fought to shake ourselves free of the soot and sadness, New Yorkers gradually returned to life as we knew it. At Caribbean Food Delights, we did the same. We had been handed a stern reminder that there was no time to delay goals and dreams. We continued to grow in business and in our commitment to philanthropy. In 2004, the Vincent HoSang Family Foundation was born, and became the banner name through which we continued to support university scholarships, community organizations, and other local institutions involved in social development programs. The suggestion for establishing the foundation had come from another one of my former teachers, the late Hon. "Rex" Nettleford, when he became vice chancellor of the University of the West Indies. I liked the suggestion immediately and acted on it. I saw this to be my family's way of saying "thank you" to the community that had embraced us, and to God for having blessed us. That year, our Foundation donated the funds needed to build a small chapel for Father Ho Lung's Missionaries of the Poor.

The following year, I had the pleasure of meeting a young Bronx dentist by the name of Dr. Roy Streete, who also wanted to make the world a better place. For several years, he and a team of some fifty amazing volunteers had been traveling to rural Jamaica twice annually to provide free dental service for the poor. Knowing that there had to be a better way to carry out his work, he was on a mission to raise funds for a mobile clinic—a bus, to be specific—that he and his team could call their own. The bus, as he explained it, would offer both dental and medical services to people who had limited access to health care. I remember the gleam in his eye as he showed me the artist's sketch at the social function at which we met. I could tell that this was a man who would stop at nothing to make his dream happen. I immediately locked into his infectious energy. I knew what he was feeling. I recognized that unmistakable drive. At the end of the function, I told him that I was going to get him his clinic on wheels. At first, he laughed as if I'd shared a really good joke. He stopped when I shook his hand, gave him my card, and told him to call me the next day to discuss the details.

I kept my word. Less than a year later, Dr. Streete and his team had their bus. Not only was it outfitted to treat dental and medical patients, it was equipped with hot and cold running water, air conditioning, and, most importantly, a bathroom. This bus now visits, among other places, my hometown of Springfield.

That summer, we took a turn on the dance floor with the franchise business. Coming up with the idea of packaging and freezing the same cooked meals we sold at Royal Caribbean Bakery, JerkQ'zine was incorporated and given an apt tagline: "A Vacation from Ordinary Food." We poured $400,000 in a flagship company-owned store in Atlanta, Georgia, where the Caribbean population was strong. As is good business practice, especially for start-ups, we included the Good Guy Clause in our lease for added protection. In the event our venture failed, we'd have the option to terminate our lease early, as long as all obligations to our landlord were made.

I remember taking stock of what we had achieved up to this point, not just in business, but also in our role as corporate citizens. The long hours, the sacrifices, the financial risk— it had all culminated in a reward that trumped being one of the world's largest producers of Jamaican patties. It gave us the chance to answer the call to moral responsibility in a significant way. We had achieved much as a business, but the Foundation made my heart sing.

Our children were now young adults. With their university studies behind them, Damian and Sabrina had taken their places in the family business, with Brian and Simone right behind. I couldn't have been happier.

In 2006, we found ourselves struggling to keep up with our orders as the demand for our products continued to nip at our heels. The expansion was going to cost some $20 million. Once again, we returned to the bank. Meanwhile, as if the stage curtains had just parted, the accolades began rolling in. Included among them was a nod of approval from a big name in business—we had been selected as one of the Forbes Small Business Enterprise Award's finalists in the food and beverage category. As thousands of entrants had tossed their hat into the ring for the country's most prestigious small business award, we were beyond humbled at the presentation ceremony, held that February at New York's iconic Lincoln Center.

It had been a long journey. Had I been asked to paint a picture reflecting our life at this point, I'd have produced a sunny day at the beach with an easy breeze and a calm sea gently washing up at our feet. But even the most beautiful beach has its share of coal-colored skies and stinging winds.

Our family was about to stand in the face of such a storm.

CHAPTER 19

Beyond explanation

"I may be a simple man, but I know enough to understand that there are some things you must accept for what it is."

Vincent

I STILL REMEMBER ONE SPRINGFIELD NIGHT IN particular. I was out in the yard with my entire family, which didn't happen often. My siblings and I were enjoying fresh fudge after our dinner—also a rare treat. We sat beneath the darkening sky, temporarily silenced as we worked at stretching out the small morsel we had each been given. Our parents sat quietly with us, although not enjoying any of the treats. They seemed content to just watch. Suddenly, my younger brother George stopped chewing, and pointed. Our eyes followed his gaze to the object of his distraction in the distance. We saw nothing but the pile of wood we stored in the yard for cooking.

"Mommy?" he said, still pointing, "Look, Mommy, there's a little girl sitting over there." My mother looked over softly, cast her eyes back to him with a wistful smile, and nodded.

"Your sister Ilene."

Decades later, my own son Damian was accompanying his mom shopping one day, when, in the middle of the department store, he stopped walking and turned to Jeanie. He was still a young boy then.

"Mom? Mom, we have to go home now." Puzzled not just by what he said but also by his urgent tone, Jeanie questioned him.

"What? Why?" she asked. "Are you feeling ill or something?"

"No, but we have to go home now. Auntie is waiting for us."

Unable to convince him that he was just imagining things, Jeanie agreed to leave. Sure enough when they pulled into the driveway, Jeanie's sister was sitting outside the house.

Sunday, May 11, 2008. The sun shone with a kind of lazy warmth on that temperate Florida day. With summer still weeks away, the humidity level was comfortably low. Jeanie, Damian, and I had been in South Florida that entire week, soaking up the great Florida weather while taking care of some personal business. As it was also Mother's Day, our plan was to fly back to New York in time to have dinner with all the kids.

That morning, Jeanie woke up looking as if she had not slept more than a couple hours. After getting dressed, she told me why. She had had a horrible dream, she said, and described the scene in which she was in a slaughterhouse filled with blood. Looking up, she saw our son Brian standing at a podium.

A couple hours later, we got the phone call no parent wants. It was from Mike, one of our managers. Mike was a close friend of Brian's, and a great guy. It was Brian, in fact, who had suggested we hire him.

At the time, Brian was splitting his time between retail at the bakery with Jeanie, and production at the plant with me. His friendly personality made him a natural at the retail end. He had a hug for just about anyone he met, which made him popular with staff and customers alike. His patience and attention to detail, however, also made him an asset in production. Once he joined the company officially, it was Brian who helped me with the tedious task of mixing the spices for the patty filling.

When I saw Mike's name on the caller ID that morning, I knew something was wrong, but assumed it was with the factory. Within seconds of hearing his tone, however, I knew the call had nothing to do with work. "Mike…? What's wrong?" His words came at me like a rush of air as he told me that Brian had been in an accident. I could tell that Mike was trying to breathe. Even though his voice told me everything I needed to know, I asked the question anyway, hoping I was wrong. "Is he OK? Is Brian all right?" I held my breath and closed my eyes, waiting for the answer. Mike paused before confirming that my son was gone. After struggling through the basic details of the accident, we hung up. I stared at the phone, forcing myself to take one breath in after the next.

I found Damian and told him what we knew: Brian had been out on his motorcycle riding with some of his friends, including Mike. While heading south on the 684 Highway, Brian hit a guardrail. The impact severed his leg, and took his life.

Damian had always been a quiet person. Even though his calm demeanor remained the same, I saw him withdrawing. I asked him to break the news to his mother while I called Sabrina. She had also been traveling that Sunday morning, and was scheduled to return just a few hours ahead of us.

Damian, Jeanie, and I barely exchanged a word as we made our way to the airport. Only an hour before, we had been hungry, and making plans for a quick lunch before flying. Instead, we bought sandwiches at the airport, but didn't even open the wrapping. Nothing could go down our throats. Quite frankly, I don't remember checking in, going through security, or even moving among other travelers. Once we boarded our flight, we each disappeared into our own dark cave. There were no tears, no words. We simply stared ahead, completely and utterly unable to think, feel, or move. All we wanted now was to go home. The rest of that day remains a blur:

"Growing up, Dad taught us to always answer the phone because you never know when it's important. I had just flown back to New York from an Atlanta business trip that morning, and could barely keep my eyes open by the time I landed. All I wanted to do was to go to my place, crawl into bed, pull the blanket over me, watch mindless television, and fall asleep. But something kept nagging at me to head to my parents' house. It was the strangest thing—a restlessness I couldn't silence. Eventually, I gave in to fatigue and headed to my place instead. Then I got Dad's call. When I heard the words *Brian's dead,* I tried to make them go away. *Why are you saying that, Dad? Stop saying that! Stop!* But no words could change it. It was at that moment that I remembered a dream I had had the week before. I saw Brian on his bike, veering off into the woods, and vanishing. I woke up the next morning feeling unsettled, but shook it off as just a bad dream. I had always heard of our family's "power" to see the future, but never did I suspect that my dream was, in fact, a premonition. Now, our free-spirited Brian was gone."

Sabrina HoSang Jordan

Sabrina immediately called Simone, surprised to hear the voicemail kick in—they had always been pretty good about the family's phone rule. After trying several times, she left the painful message for her sister:

"That week, while my parents and Damian were in Florida, I came in from the city, where I was living, to hang out with Brian. At the time, he was still at home, and had taken up residency in the basement. That week, we talked a lot and just enjoyed each other's company. On Saturday, when I visited him at the retail store, he insisted I stay and learn how to operate the cash register. 'You never know when we might need you,' he said. Early that Sunday morning, I woke up to the sound of the doorbell—it was Brian's riding crew, ready for their ride to Connecticut. I kissed my brother on his cheek, as he got ready to leave. 'Ride safe,' I said. 'Love you.'

"Our plan for later that day was to surprise Mom with a clean kitchen and basket of health products—Brian and I were into health and wellness, and thought it would make for a great gift. So I got ready and drove to the local health food store. When I finished shopping, I returned to my car, realizing only then that I had accidentally left my phone on the seat. I saw that I had several missed messages, not my usual phone activity for a Sunday morning. I frowned as I began to check them. That's when I heard Sabrina's frantic voice, 'Brian's dead! Brian's dead!'

"After Mike gave me their exact location, my heart pounding like an angry fist, I stopped on the way to grab a friend who knew how to get there quickly. But I still had one frustrating detail to take care of before rushing to Brian's side—I had to get gas. My tank could not get me there. That's when I heard Dad's gentle reminder: *never let your tank drop below a quarter.* By the time I arrived, Sabrina was already there, crying hysterically. Eventually, the police escorted us over to Brian's lifeless body. I was relieved my parents were not there—this was not something they needed to see.

"After Brian's death, I spent a year helping at the retail store."

Simone HoSang

After contacting Simone, Sabrina then reached out to someone she knew I would want to see at a time like this— Father Mac:

"I was home that Sunday when Sabrina called about Brian. When she said the words, I immediately got upset with her. I told her that she was speaking nonsense, as I had only just seen Brian two weeks before, and even reminded him that the bike he was riding had only two wheels, and that he should therefore be careful. 'Father,' he said with his huge smile, which he followed up with one of his reassuring hugs, 'don't worry. I can handle this.'

"With my heart lodged in my throat, I called Vinnie. They were still at the airport in Fort Lauderdale, about to catch their flight. He was calm, but clearly in shock. I turned to my wife and told her that I could not allow Vinnie and his family to travel back alone from JFK in a taxi. They needed to be with friends. I called another old high-school friend of his, and together we met them at JFK with two cars. 'I don't even know what to say to you guys,' I said as I embraced them. I had no words. But I could sense that Vinnie wanted to talk with me privately, so I asked the other friend to take Jeanie and Damian home while I rode with Vinnie.

"Once inside my car, Vinnie seemed to exhale both physically and emotionally. He did not shout, curse, blame or damn anyone or anything. There was not even a hint of bitterness at life, or at God, but I could see that this man—this father—was hurting. In the years leading up to this point, Brian was always with him—and had almost become Vincent's understudy. In a steady but vulnerable voice, Vinnie asked me the question that mattered most to him. 'Father Mac, what about his soul? Is his soul OK?' He would ask me this several times on that drive. I told him what I believed—that his soul was now in God's hands.

"I went with Vinnie to identify Brian's body. It didn't even look like him. Two weeks before I was laughing with this young man, this beacon of life. Now I stood next to his still body, giving him his last rites. I wept the entire way through.

"Up to that point, I had always felt that Vinnie was a man of God—privately and deeply. That day confirmed that I was right. I witnessed a man accepting God's will without question. By the time we got to his house, Vincent was asking me to take over the funeral arrangements. 'Father, I have no experience with this. Please. I don't know what to do.' And so I took over everything. The church we got was a large one, but still wasn't large enough. Everyone wanted to be there for the family.

"After the funeral, Vinnie asked me what he could do in his son's memory that would be of benefit to others. I told him that the music program I ran at the church was in need of a piano and organ, so he bought a lovely two-in-one piano and organ piece, and put Brian's name on it. Today, that beautiful instrument brings joy to the instructors and students making music with it. The family would also establish a college scholarship in his memory. I know both gestures have given Vinnie and his family some small measure of peace."

Rev. Canon Calvin McIntyre
Rector, Church of the
Good Shepherd

"When Vincent called and told me what had happened to his son, I heard no self-pity from him. When he asked if I'd come for the service, I didn't hesitate to say yes. He seemed to want that fellowship, so I stayed at his house. Jeanie, his wife, was taking it badly. Vincent remained then, as he had been on the phone earlier—conscious and thoughtful. In our quiet conversations, he spoke positively about the way his son had grown into a fine young man. There was no anger, only love. I saw by the way he reacted that he was a man completely at peace. Instead of sinking into despair, he sank into his faith."

Very Rev. Fr. Richard Ho Lung, MOP

I don't assume that I'm going to be exempted from hurt just because I'm a man of faith. Worse has happened to others. All we can do is accept our blows with grace. That's why, even though I am a planner, I still remind myself to savor life one precious day at a time.

Losing our Brian was like witnessing all that was logical and beautiful in this world disappear into a hellish vortex. I had not, until this point, known pain like that. Being separated from my family as a young boy had been one kind of anguish. Losing my child was like having all the joy I had ever known gush out of my soul like a broken water main. It was just not in me to rail against God, however. The way I saw it, God had been good to me all along. I could not then turn around and be a fair-weather friend because I was angry about something that had gone terribly wrong. No amount of rage or anger was going to bring our Brian back to us. All I could do was trust that this had to be. So, I told myself what I believed—that my son was now in the hands of another loving father.

In the months that followed, we pulled ourselves up in our own way, and in our own time. It took more effort than we could ever have imagined, but we woke up each day forcing ourselves to move forward as a family, as a business, and as members of the human race.

CHAPTER 20

Here today looking at tomorrow

"When it comes to going after your share of the market, I say *live, but let others live too.* There's enough pie to go around. If I were to eat it all, I'd probably choke or get a serious case of indigestion."

Vincent

OUR FAMILY—OUR TEAM—WAS DOWN BY ONE. Moving forward was the only action I knew. Self-pity had never been a part of my being. Not only is it unproductive, my life had never had room for that kind of luxury. Thankfully, the old adage that "life goes on" is true. At some point, the same train that had flattened me only weeks before, slowed down just enough for me to climb aboard again. I held on tight as it picked up speed, the ache in my heart still like lead.

It was now mid-2008, and we had much to do. First on the list was closing JerkQ'zine's doors. After a three-year test run, the diagnosis was simple: it was low on viability. With both sides protected by the Good Guy clause—signed in our company's name of course—we were able to terminate the lease with our landlord prematurely, without any drama.

Perhaps we should have given the franchise venture a longer warm-up period, but my instincts told me otherwise. The food was tasty, that much we knew. The price for the five-pound tray was also fair, that much we had ensured. But, try as we did, we could not generate the sales a franchisee would need to turn a profit. I believe the issue was a cultural one. Caribbean people, on a whole, prefer having their meals served fresh off the stovetop. (I admit to sharing this preference.) Clearly, we underestimated this point by thinking that the need for convenience in hectic America would eclipse this Caribbean partiality. So, when prospective franchisees began expressing interest, I had to tell them the truth. I told them that, based on our figures, JerkQ'zine could not promise a life of private schools for their children, fancy vacations, and luxury homes and cars for their families. I put numbers to paper each time to make my point. I told them that unless they could make a certain minimum, I was not going to take their money. I saw this as a two-way street. When you spend your money with Vincent HoSang, I told them, we both have to be happy.

Fortunately, our main line of business was much healthier. Almost as if on cue, the following year we were once again considering expansion. Our patties were doing better than we could have hoped for with the main club stores. In fact, we were in a perpetual race to fill their orders.

It was a happy challenge to have. Now with ample land on which to expand, we could build to our heart's content. I decided to embrace technology. This time, we installed an entirely new third line that was about 90 percent automated. This genius feat of engineering took the product from start to finish: mixing, sheeting, baking, cooling, and freezing, then on to X-raying and packaging. About the only thing it didn't do was deliver the orders to our customers. I threw myself into the well-timed distraction. By the end of the project, we had grown to become a plant ready to tackle the market with over 100,000 square feet of pure production power. By now, we were offering our customers even more variety: patties made with beef, chicken, or vegetarian fillings. Our volume output had also reached a new level. Now we had the capacity to produce 40,000 patties an hour. I had long been a fan of engineering and modern technology. The decision to dig our heels in deeper in this direction was, as far as I could see, inevitable.

Look around you when trying to take the temperature of a certain market. The price of bread tells me a lot. I've noticed, for instance, that the same loaf that used to go for $4 is now often on sale at half the price. This tells me two things: one, that bread has peaked at a certain price, and, two, that manufacturers' profit margins are being crushed. These are the signs that make a business owner pace the floor. This is also the reason why automation is a manufacturer's friend.

When one door closes, they say, another opens. In 2008, BJ's Wholesale Club approached us about coming up with another product. It was the magic question any businessman wants to hear. *What else do you have to offer?* This time they wanted something with a wider appeal. What about trying a classic comfort food this time? How about chicken pot pie? We had to admit, it made perfect sense. David Cybul, my faithful sounding board, also thought it was a brilliant idea. Chicken pot pie could easily be described as the more popular, less risqué, cousin to the Jamaican patty. We didn't even eat pot pies in our home, but that didn't faze me. Entering unfamiliar territory made me all the more determined to work harder at it. I admit, however, that the thought of making a go for the mainstream market felt a bit like going after a girl you know to be beyond your reach. I had always wanted to include the wider market in our scope of production—I just didn't know how. Now that the opportunity had presented itself, the temptation to try was an itch I just had to scratch. With high expectations, we donned our gowns and hairnets, and began the process of developing something new and wonderful.

Our first attempt soared like a deflated balloon. The filling was as satisfying as bland cornbread—it delivered on looks, but not on taste. If that wasn't bad enough, the crust was far too flaky. We decided against setting a deadline and rushing the process. The right product required the right amount of time.

It was at about this time that we responded to another gauntlet that had been thrown at our feet, this time by the United States Department of Health. The issue at hand was the elimination of trans fat. Now, more than ever, healthy foods were in demand, even in fast-food-hungry America. For those of us in the relatively small Jamaican patty industry, it pretty much meant one thing if we wanted to join the revolution: cutting out the suet. The hard fat that surrounds a cow's kidneys, this ingredient had long been the secret behind transforming an otherwise forgettable crust into a beautifully flaky experience. I almost chuckled when the mandate came around. Some ten years before, one of our customers had issued the friendly challenge that we consider a substitute for the sinful suet. "It would make for a healthier patty," Dr. Rainford said one day while picking up his usual order. As he was a medical doctor, I knew his advice was coming from a good place, but it felt like being asked to bake a cake without flour.

I have since learned that there is such a thing as a flourless cake, and that our patties can pass the taste and flake tests without the naughty suet. While we could have continued to use a small amount of suet and remain compliant with the new regulations, we decided to do away with it altogether.

The months marched on. In keeping with our promise to give back, we forged ahead with new charity outreach plans. This time we were shaking hands with the Jamaican government on our foundation's commitment to help raise funds for cancer-screening machines for two hospitals, one in Kingston, and one in Montego Bay. The Montego Bay hospital was the same one in which I had had my appendectomy as a kid. A long-term project meant to rally the support of the Jamaican diaspora in the New York area, the final check would also not be ready for another few years.

Meanwhile, the company began receiving accolades of different kinds, all indicating that we had "done well" either as a business or corporate citizen. We received each with grateful smiles and full hearts. You never really grow tired of hearing that you've made a difference, or that you've done outstanding work, even if you've been at it for decades. Among the nods of approval was one by a French company. After touring our plant, its representatives indicated that we were the kind of operation they were looking for to produce their croissants. I took this as the ultimate compliment. There is something special about receiving such a thumbs up from an industry counterpart—someone who has walked your path and knows exactly what the markers of excellence are in that particular arena.

While we discussed the possibility of working with them, I knew that this was not the direction I wanted to take. I admit to questioning my hesitation at the time. This was an excellent opportunity. These were good people—seasoned in the field. Why was I not jumping at this? I didn't fight myself on the issue for long, however. By now I was in my early seventies. I had learned to heed my gut instincts. I didn't know the exact reason behind my hesitation then, but I knew it would make itself known in time. In the end I declined the offer. We would not be their manufacturers, but we wished them every success in their search for one.

Later that fall, not long after I turned seventy-two, an envelope arrived from the University of the West Indies, addressed to me. I unfolded the letter and smiled. The university wished to acknowledge my philanthropic efforts with an honorary Doctor of Laws (LLD). I, along with the other nominees, would be conferred with the honor on the occasion of that year's graduation ceremony at the Mona campus, located in Kingston. I booked my ticket for the trip back to school.

It was one of those days you take for granted when you live in the tropics, but that remains imprinted on your mind once you've left its shores—a blue sky with gentle swaths of light clouds. It was December, a time when the trade winds bring cooler temperatures, and the sun feels assertive but gentle. It was the kind of day I had known as a boy in Springfield.

That afternoon, December 12, 2012, we all gathered under a massive tent on the expansive green lawn of that university's beautiful campus. As the ceremony unfolded, I immersed myself in the moment, enjoying the thrill of wearing a cap and gown. For me, recognition for a life of giving was like being handed a gift you're not expecting. You want to pull the bows off, rip apart the colorful paper, and get to the contents of the box. At the same time, you want to stare at it, shake it, guess what's inside. You want the moment to last forever.

Later that night, I relaxed quietly in my hotel room, my mind roaming over the day's events: the congratulatory handshakes, the photographers, the busy chatter, smiling faces offering heartfelt words of gratitude. I reminisced, playing the reel of my life as it had unfolded over the decades, humbled that God had thought me worthy of so many blessings.

I saw myself delivering scrap paper in a van that had just run out of gas. I felt the cold winter night slicing through my body as I crouched on a porch for shelter and strength. I went back to the long days and short nights, the years of saving pennies, and the life of relentless sacrifice. I smiled knowingly at the moments when I felt like a defective product coming off of an equally defective conveyor belt—and the moments when I wondered if I'd go careening over the sheer cliff.

Then a certain image flashes before me, and stays.

It is gray, a little shaky, but it is so real I can almost touch it.

I am with my father in front of our little shop in Springfield. It has just rained. The air is fresh. A light breeze sweeps by us. He is waiting for customers to come in, hoping that they will buy our goods so that maybe he can buy shoes for his children. I'm standing next to him, sharing in his wish for more customers, and a better life. His face says he's tired—so tired—but his gaze says he has hope. It says he believes in me. It lingers on his face because I have just told him that, someday, I'll become a doctor.

EPILOGUE

AS I MAKE THE FINISHING TOUCHES TO MY STORY,
I can't help but share in the worn-out observation that the older
I get, the faster time passes. For the record, I find this irritating.
I may not spring out of bed as quickly or as early as I used to,
but I am far from ready to cut my days in half, take longer vaca-
tions, or shy away from new challenges.

Construction on the business we built from the ground
up has not stopped. When BJ's suggested we come up with a
new product for their customers back in 2008, we embraced
the opportunity to prove ourselves in a new arena. Once again,
we opened ourselves up to risk, took initiative, and set out to
make it work. The venture had its share of challenges. When our

first attempts resulted in an unsatisfactory product, we continued working on it but allowed other production to temporarily distract us. Between 2013 and 2014, we returned to the pot pies, improved the formula, and waited as BJ's Wholesale Club tested them for six months. Today, you can find our chicken pot pies in several BJ's stores.

Producing an item that meets the approval of the mainstream market is, at least for *this* American immigrant, the realization of the impossible dream. It is early in the game, of course, but we're encouraged by the response, not just from the end consumer, but from our own wholesale customers, who continue to see us for what we are: a reliable producer of quality food.

I have decided to expand the plant one last time before handing the reins over to the next generation. Naturally, we will go borrowing again. I am the first to admit that some think I'm certifiably insane for taking on more risk in my golden years. Maybe they're right. Maybe I need to buy a boat and go fishing, something I love to do. The thing is, I'm not ready to cruise just yet. I'm still having fun. What's more, this time we're in a different position. Now that we've proven ourselves, repeatedly, borrowing has become a whole lot easier. I even get calls (at least one a week) with offers to buy our company. *You're the kind of tip-top business our clients are looking for,* the caller usually says. I am humbled by each offer. Each one reminds me that we have built something good. Our company may not be the biggest nor even the best, but it's good enough to have others craning their necks and paying attention.

As our philanthropic work continues, I grow increasingly proud of my children for embracing this way of life. As a parent, I think it's important that the next generation be raised to feel compassion for others. I include my children as often as I can in our efforts. Recently, for instance, we were instrumental in a joint Caribbean Food Delights/Jamaican Diaspora in New York initiative to raise funds to assist with the purchase of two Linear Accelerator ("LINAC") cancer machines for the Cornwall Regional and the Kingston Public Hospitals in Jamaica. The money raised was handed over to the Ministry of Health of Jamaica in 2014. The following year, we rallied once again around our island home after the Ebola virus outbreak in West Africa. In an effort to secure the country's port of entry, the Jamaica Consulate in New York spearheaded the Ebola Prevention Programme, which saw us donating a walk-through fever-sensing unit to Kingston's Norman Manley International Airport. In October of the same year, much to my surprise and delight, I was blessed with the conferment of the national honor, the Order of Jamaica, for philanthropic and dedicated service to the Jamaican Diaspora and Jamaica. Of all our charity ventures, however, my sentimental favorite remains the mobile health clinic. It came far too late to help our old friends, but I take solace in the hope that it is now helping their children and grandchildren.

I remain eternally grateful for all who came into my life. Without them, there may not have been a story to tell. At the top of the list are my wife and children, of course. My family has been my biggest driver in just about everything I have done, and continue to do. I know I have not always been the easiest person to live with, but I'm glad they're the crew aboard my ship. I hope this book has helped to shed some light on why I have lived my life a certain way.

My staff and managers are the bright sparks that make going to work every day a true joy. Many have that "right attitude" I have spoken so much about. We would not be the success we are today were it not for some of the exceptional men and women who have come through our doors.

Our customers remain my other source of joy. Some have been with us from the start when we were but a tiny bakery. Others have joined us along the way. Most have stayed. To this day, I still answer my calls, and I still smile when there's a customer on the line telling us that we have outdone ourselves, or missed the mark. These faithful followers have always believed in our brand and have never let us forget that we have a reputation to uphold. They don't want to see us slip. That's true customer loyalty. I hope other business owners are just as blessed to have such strict inspectors.

I remain eternally grateful for the friends who gave their support, professionalism, and camaraderie. I will forever be grateful for the Frankies, the Lynns, the Davids, the Toms, the

Allans, and all those who gave me a shoulder to lean on, or even stand on. Some are no longer with us, but I will forever remember them as honorable men and women, kind human beings, and true friends. I am also grateful for those who showed up in my life as hurdles. I believe God sent them to strengthen me, and to teach me how to overcome them. Because of them, I learned a lot about myself.

I end this story with my family of origin. We never did reunite since that day we left Springfield. Perhaps my parents thought it best to leave well enough alone out of respect for the years that had wedged themselves between us, and for the families that adopted their children. I'll never know. It may count for little, but we at least knew where each sibling lived, and how each was doing in general.

For the most part, we did the best we could with our lives. Yuklin, the oldest, lived out her life in Montego Bay. She passed away in 2008. Even though Que never changed his carefree ways, he seemed happy with his life, which is a comfort to the rest of us. When Que entered his senior years, King, Nuke, George, and I bought him a small home in the countryside, so he could live out his golden years quietly and worry-free, which he did until his death in 2000. My sister Mae, the lucky winner of that raffle prize so long ago, ended up making her life in Kingston, where she married and had a son and a daughter. She would leave us earlier, in 1990. Today, her son, Garrick, is a successful businessman. He lives only thirty minutes away from me.

After decades of working and building a life, King left Jamaica for the States. He is now retired in Arizona, where he lives with his devoted wife, Carmen. A brain aneurysm some years ago robbed him of his ability to speak, but that doesn't stop us from communicating. We still "speak" almost weekly, with Carmen acting as interpreter. The brother who had always stood by my side is still with me. I don't make a move without filling him in on the details.

Nuke continues to live a happy and prosperous life in Montego Bay with her husband, Ken. We still speak regularly, and see each other when we can. George now lives in Kingston, where he enjoys success in several businesses. Winston, the youngest sibling, works with us at the Mount Vernon bakery in the accounts department. I'm grateful he's with us. It's something special to have the witnesses of your youth close by—it's a privilege few get to enjoy. As for our three half-brothers, they have all passed on. While I got to know them only briefly in my early twenties, one would form a close bond with George, even becoming business partners with him.

As for Aunt Sylvia, I continued to look after her as I did since the day Uncle Harrison died. I'd like to think that I helped her live comfortably, as she had done for me in our short time as a family. My second mother passed away in 2014.

Some say that I have never looked back since I left the dirt roads of Springfield. In a way it's true—I never did allow my beginning to determine my end. I did allow it, however, to influence my journey for the better. While I hope that our philanthropic work continues to bring some relief to those in whose shoes I once walked, I hope that my story brings hope to those searching for a way out on their own terms. The life of an entrepreneur is not for everyone. In fairness to today's generation, I acknowledge that times have changed. New rules and regulations and an increasingly competitive market have made it a different arena now.

That said, I believe the old tenets remain the same: Visualize your dream and know it like you know your own skin. Gather ample supplies of faith, perseverance, and patience. Stay focused. Most importantly, work hard. When I started out, several people wondered if I'd make it. As they pointed out, I was neither a baker nor a cook. They were right. Matter of fact, they still are.

Above all, live your life to its fullest potential. Whether your wish is to build a stellar career, or build something of your own, make the most of your precious God-given talent. Develop and practice rituals that feed your spirit. I still go down on one knee each morning to state my hopes, intentions, and gratitude. I'll even do this in the office when the spirit moves me.

As for those pennies on the sidewalk, I still stop to pick them up. Why? For one, it keeps me nimble. I consider it a point of pride that, at my age, I can still bend my knees and straighten up with neither help nor hesitation. The other reason is nostalgic.

Once upon a time, I saw those lost or discarded copper pieces as part of my journey—a means to a better end. Once upon a time, those pennies made a difference. They led me to a job. The job led to a steady income. The income led to savings. The savings led to an investment in my future. The rest, as they say, is history. Today, when I see those coins at my feet, they remind me that even the smallest of steps can lead to something magnificent and wonderful. That is why, for as long as my body allows, I will always reach for them.

Vincent Getchun HoSang,

O.J., O.D.